A History of Warrington

Previously published as
Warrington - A Heritage

Harry Boscow

P & D Riley

First published as *Warrington - A Heritage* in 1943

This reset and illustrated edition first published 1997 by
P & D Riley (Publishers)
12 Bridgeway East,
Runcorn,
Cheshire WA7 6LD

ISBN: 1 874712 24 7

British Library Cataloguing - in - Publication Data
A Catalogue Record for this book is available from the British Library

Printed in England by Redwood Books, Wiltshire.

Cover picture: Land Army Girls in Warrington in World War II.

Introduction

Warrington was once described as a county borough and market town of Lancashire, (now Cheshire), situated approximately 180 miles from London served by the London and North Eastern, Great Western & London, Midland & Scottish Railways, as well as the Cheshire Lines Railway and was a busy industrial centre with a population in 1931 of 79,317.

Since then, of course, things have changed. The town still boasts some heavy industry and, thankfully, two railways but population figures have soared in the past three decades.

Warrington is also at the centre of a major motorway network and is fast becoming a service provider town which balances with its remaining industrial heritage. Warrington is no longer in its traditional county, but is now a town in Cheshire following a border re-structuring which took place in the 1970s.

One thing which hasn't changed, however, is Warrington's long and fascinating history which dates back more than two thousand years, and in this work Harry Boscow succinctly sums up the town's past.

Peter Riley

About the Author

Harry Boscow was born in 1911 and after education in the area he attended college in London between 1930 and 1932, prior to taking up a post as Geography teacher at Beamont Boys School. He married in 1938, just prior to World War II and in 1942 he joined the RAF and was based in Hereford and Lincolnshire, being demobbed in 1946 and returning to Beamont. In 1958 he became head of St. Mark's Junior and Infants school in Bolton, returning to Warrington as head of St. James' in 1961. In 1966 he took on his final headship at St Werburgh's school from which he retired 10 years later. A keen member of Warrington Photographic Society, Mr Boscow died in 1992. His widow Dorothea still lives in Warrington.

Contents

Horse breeders and sellers were a common sight in old Warrington and local hostelries took great pride in providing superior stabling facilities for visitors to the town, and pictured outside the Seven Stars Inn is landlord William Brown with one of his proud beasts

PREFACE

This is the story of a town, our town. There have been, at various times, quite a few books, and many papers, written on various aspects of it, but none of its whole story. This is an attempt to present that whole picture. It began when Mr. Morgan James, Headmaster of Beamont Senior Boys' School, showed me that any teaching of geography and history should begin with the child's own district, and crystallised in thoughtful moments whilst away, except for leave periods, on service with the forces.

It became for me not just a school book but the Saga of my town. Its inheritance to its people through the ages, and their contribution to its living life. In such a way I have tried to tell the tale, not glossing over its black spots, nor polishing its bright ones. Just a plain unvarnished story that came to represent the reason for my present absence from its life, just as the life of thousands of other towns and villages coalescing into this England is the reason why all of us are fighting today.

To the work of those other writers I am indebted a great deal. A full list of authorities will be found at the end. To the staffs of the Warrington Museum and Library I must record my thanks for their courtesy and help while the ground work was being dug.

Acknowledgements

The publishers would like to thank the following for their invaluable help in the preparation of this edition

Mrs Dorothea Boscow, widow of the author, for giving permission to reproduce the original book in this new format and for her enthusiasm for the project

Warrington Library and Museum for supplying illustrations

Ken Bryan for supplying illustrations

Olive Watkin for supplying the cover photograph

Aquarius Publications for supplying illustrations

Chapter I
Prehistoric Warrington

Warrington, situated as it is on the River Mersey, halfway between Liverpool and Manchester, is aptly described today as "The Gateway to Lancashire." As such a gateway is its past and present importance due. The map shows us that to the north of the river the land is flat. Southwards it rises fairly steeply to two hundred feet, the main features being the scarp of Hill Cliff and the wooded folds of the land. Southwards one enters the smiling· county of Cheshire, northwards the smoke and slag heaps of Lancashire.

To the south of the town, the hundred foot contour line approaches fairly close to the river. Northwards it bends back away from the Mersey. The Mersey itself is fringed with marshes, many of them very old, which have hampered communications, and even today to some extent, offer an obstacle to human intercourse. The present configuration of the landscape of the area surrounding the town is the result of vast happenings and upheavals of long ago.

The district first comes into view in what the geologists call Triassic times.

At this period, large parts of Lancashire and Cheshire were under water, and on the floor of this Triassic Sea there was laid down the debris brought by the rivers flowing into it from the adjacent uplands. This deposit, through years of accumulation, formed itself into the rocks of the New Red Sandstone. During this period the great salt deposits of Cheshire were formed, which, throughout the years of man's occupation, have influenced the life of the district.

Later, the basic landscape in more or less its present form was thrown up, consequent upon the gigantic earth movements which brought into being

9

Navvies at work digging the Manchester Ship Canal

the Alps. These movements, spreading outwards like ripples on a pond, caused the floor of the Triassic rocks to split up into the plateau and valleys we know so well today.

We must bear in mind that right from these early times the district was a plain between two highland masses, the Welsh Highlands and the Pennines, and that our belts of high ground formed a connecting link between them. This fact has had a great bearing upon the evolution of the district.

The surface details of the land about us are not the result of that upheaval of Triassic times, but the collective result of happenings since then. By the end of that epoch, our district, as we have seen, was made up of sandstone rocks. Then came that remarkable change known as the Ice Age. As a result of climatic changes, the weather grew colder, with the result that vast ice sheets were formed on the highlands surrounding our district, namely the Pennines, the Welsh Highlands and the Lake District.

These vast glaciers moved downwards and coalesced in the basin of the Irish Sea, whence they moved southwards as a vast sheet of ice, often more than a thousand feet thick, invading and overriding our district and advancing many miles to the south of us. Naturally the two highland masses on either side of us concentrated the maximum eroding effort of the ice on our lower lying district. Great thicknesses of rock were scraped off, and this mass of debris was accumulated on, under, and in the ice sheet as a mass of clay, mostly made up of the sandstones of the district, but also containing boulders brought from the Lake District, Wales and the Pennines. This mass of clay blocked the valleys and covered the landscape, completely transforming the surface.

A great deal of the surface of our district is covered with this boulder clay formed in the Ice Age. As an example, when the Manchester Ship Canal was being cut, from six to sixteen feet of this clay had to be removed before the solid rock was found.

Towards the end of the Ice Age, when the climate changed and the ice melted, vast quantities of water formed over the Cheshire Plain, draining away by means of our river and others in Cheshire to the Irish Sea. These waters carried with them quantites of sand and gravels, which were deposited adjacent to their courses, so that the boulder clay was covered by them. Since those times, the wind, rain, and frosts have been at work upon the surface left by the ice sheets, until it has been eroded and moulded into the forms and shapes with which we are familiar today.

The vegetation which developed on this surface had a direct effect upon any animal or human being inhabiting the region in those far-off times.

Immediately following the Ice Age, only such plants and animals adapted to a cold climate survived. Such trees as birch, pine, and tundra scrub grew on the higher land to the north and south of us, for the river valley was still a swampy mass. Such animals as the great hairy mammoth, the Arctic fox, reindeer, hippopotamus, sabre-toothed tiger, and woolly rhinoceros no doubt roamed the district, for some discoveries of their bones have been found, as for example, when excavating a sand pit at Bob's Bridge, between here and Runcorn, a magnificent pair of deer antlers were found. Also at Creswell Crags in Derbyshire, excavators have discovered numerous traces of many of these animals.

It was at this period that our earliest ancestors first made their appearance in England. All the evidence points to their coming from Europe, across land (where now is the Straits of Dover) by which England at that time was joined to the continent. Naturally they would be most numerous in southern England, though probably very thinly dispersed over the countryside.

These early men and women whom the archaeologists called Palæolithic Man, were hunters and nomads, always wandering after wild animals and searching for a more plentiful supply of roots, shoots, nuts and berries to add variety to their diet.

No doubt in their wanderings some of these early people penetrated northwards and roamed about our district, but they left little trace of themselves in the neighbourhood.

The gathering of roots and vegetable food was largely the task of the women folk. Hunting game and fur-bearing animals was the man's job. As the little communities were not numerically strong, probably consisting of a family or two wandering along together, a direct attack on their prey was impossible. Therefore they had to devise numerous indirect methods. Traps would be set on the trails which led to watering holes, or they would drive the animals over some steep escarpment, and there they would feast on the bodies, everyone eating his fill, for a long time might elapse before they could eat again. The chase was uncertain, so they made the most of their opportunities.

Our knowledge of these early people comes to us from their implements, their habitations, and their burial sites. In this district, little definite trace of any kind has been found. We know that their implements were of stone and flint in the shape of axes. The people themselves were primitive in the extreme, making use of caves, or shelter given by overhanging cliffs. The nearest places to our district where habitable sites have been found, are at Creswell Crags in Derbyshire, and Ffynnon Beuno and Cae Gwyn near St. Asaph in the Vale of Clwyd. As no burial sites have been discovered in our district, we must conclude that in those early Palæolithic times, the Mersey Valley and the plains of Lancashire and Cheshire were not inhabited, though it is possible they were hunting grounds for communities settled elsewhere. Small groups, more venturesome than the rest, might have followed the higher ground instead of the swampy river valley in their eternal quest for food.

This period of contacts lasted a tremendous number of years. The end of this early period of Man was accompanied by considerable climatic changes, during which the cold semi-arctic conditions prevailing after the Ice Age gave way to warmer days. The approximate date of this new epoch is given as about 9,500 to 8,000 B.C.

This change of climate would naturally be reflected in a change of vegetation over the area. The tundra type was gradually replaced by a more luxuriant forest growth of willow, birch and pine. The resulting new environment in which these early people now found themselves living would naturally force them to alter their mode of life.

Hunters they still remained, but their weapons improved. This new period, known as the Mesolithic period, saw the introduction of flint headed lances and arrows. These were adaptations of the older types of weapons, as well as the result of a new influx of culture from the continent.

Naturally, with the change in climate and vegetation, the animal life altered as well. Instead of fur-bearing animals, the red deer, wild pig and elk were hunted by the mesolithic folk.

They were mostly cave dwellers, especially during the winter months. Finds of small flints have been made at Creswell Crags, Alderley Edge, and at the Red Noses, New Brighton. There is some evidence, too, to show that this period probably saw the emergence of artificially constructed dwellings. On the Pennines, round patches of flints have been found with nearby traces of a hearth which sometimes shows burnt birch branches. Probably some early flint craftsman had a crude erection of branches and

13

leaves to shelter him as he plied his craft. One such chipping floor has also been found near our district at Alderley Edge and at Prestatyn.

In Southern England, where caves were not so easy to find, they constructed dwellings more or less in the form of a shallow pit roofed over with twigs and branches.

Very few traces of these Mesolithic people exist in our district or in Cheshire, but though it cannot be proved that they lived in this area, they most probably visited it and hunted in its forests. During this period, great geographical changes took place, as our country was separated from the continent and became an island, and more important perhaps, the great North Sea was formed.

Towards the end of the Mesolithic period, new arrivals to our country from the continent brought a new culture and a new mode of life. As the weather was becoming warmer, the hardier nomadic tribes moved northward, and the weaker ones left in the south were easily replaced by the new people from the continent.

These people, arriving by dug-out canoe, were herdsmen, rearing cattle, sheep and goats, and tilling the fields, with the result that the communities settled down close to their fields and flocks instead of wandering about the countryside with no fixed abode. They constructed circular settlements on hill tops, and commenced making pottery of a crude type, mining flints and polishing stones to form wedge-shaped axes. The new age which was thus dawning has been given the name of Neolithic or New Stone Age. Gradually these Neolithic people became bolder and paddled in their canoes not only across the Channel to England, but even across the North Sea to the shores of Yorkshire, and up the west coast to Wales and Northern Ireland, eventually arriving at the Pennines by journeys from Wales. Yorkshire, and the south.

As forests covered the country below the 500ft. contour, their journeys would be along the higher ground, and they gradually penetrated the country along ancient trackways running along the ridge of downs and hills.

It has been proved that our district became a route joining the highlands of Wales with those of the Pennines and Yorkshire Wolds. A series of

A sketch of old Warrington

scattered finds of implements in our district, when plotted on a map, form a link, like milestones along a road connecting the settlements of the west with those of the east. These finds also prove that in all probability these movements were carried out with a definite purpose, such as trading in implements, or finding a new settlement.

At Penmaenmawr, in North Wales, a site has been found where these implements of stone and flint were made, and axes made from this stone have been found in Cheshire, Yorkshire and the Pennines. Perhaps they were carried there by traders, or journeys were made to North Wales to obtain these implements. Some were probably lost on the way, and by these discoveries we are able to trace the routes taken on their wanderings.

From Wales and Chester, routes lead via Tarporley and Eddisbury Hill to the Peak. They can also be traced along the southern banks of the Mersey and Irwell to the Calder, and so into Yorkshire. Traces of routes on both sides of the river at Warrington indicate that a crossing of this obstacle could be made here. Thus the future position of our town begins to appear, for once it was found possible to cross the river at this point, it would naturally become the focus of routes on either side of the river, and would be used more frequently as time went by.

What kind of people were these Neolithic folk? Archæologists say they are of Mediterranean stock, short, dark people with long, narrow skulls, oval faces, retreating jaws and a narrow forehead. They used flint tools, the most common being axes or celts, varying

Stone hammer

from a few inches to one foot three inches in length. The axes were often driven into the wooden handle and bound into place. Flint scrapers were made of flint and used for cleaning animal skins or for shaping wood.

Specimens of these axes can be seen in the Museum, as some have been discovered at Tarporley, Acton Brook, Orford, Stockton Heath, Eddisbury Hill and Helsby.

Perforated implements were developed too, stone axes with holes through them for better attachment to the shaft, and at Stockton Heath two axe hammers were discovered. At Hill Cliff a small pebble hammer was found. Many finds were made in Cheshire, including Beeston Castle, Birkenhead, Cheadle, Gatley, Liscard, Moreton Old Hall, New Brighton, Tarporley and Weston Point, and at Newton-le-Willows, Winwick and Haydock in Lancashire. The map shows these discoveries plotted in relation to the large centres of settlement and to the nature of the country at that time. They used these tools to shape spear shafts, dig out canoes and even to mine flints. With them they also built their houses, but no traces of dwellings have been found in our district. Their houses, similar to those built by the Mesolithic people, later developed into a building with low stone walls and a porch.

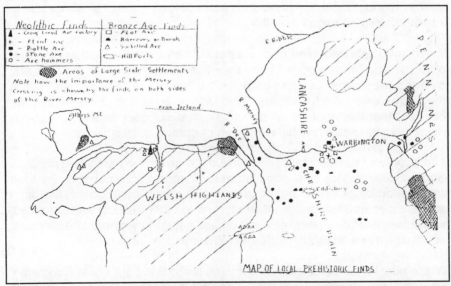

MAP OF LOCAL PREHISTORIC FINDS

The flint scrapers suggest skin clothing, probably sewn together with animal sinews and a crude form of bone needle. With axes of some kind they probably tilled a small patch of ground close to their dwelling, cutting the corn with a stone sickle and grinding it between two stones.

Primarily though, they were herdsmen. They had domesticated the dog, and used him no doubt in helping to handle their few oxen or urus. A perfect skull of the urus was found at Walton Lock when cutting for the Ship Canal was in progress. Two dug-out canoes which are on show in the Museum were found at the same time. Whether these canoes belong to this period or one later is not definitely known, and so we shall leave a more detailed discussion until later on.

Sometimes these primitive dwellings were grouped together and protected by a ditch and rampart or by a palisade. This wall not only protected the community but also their livestock from wolves and other wild animals. These were the forerunners of the hill-forts of later times.

A simple form of pottery was developed and used for domestic purposes, and probably for storing seeds of grain. But it was in mining material for their tools that we see the Neolithic people at their best. Men of the previous ages, constantly on the move, gathered material from the surface as they found it. These people, now more settled in their habits, dug deep into the chalk and mined their flints.

The most celebrated mine of all was at Grimes Caves in Norfolk, a model of which is in the Museum. Here they dug through ten feet of sand, and quarried twenty feet of chalk to get at the main seam of flint, after which they cut tunnels and galleries. This was a remarkable feat when we consider that their tools were only picks made of deer antlers, or spades made from the shoulder blades of oxen or crudely cut from wood.

The people of the Neolithic period are often given the name Megalithic or Stone Builders. Besides using stones for tools, they constructed their religious buildings and burial chambers of stone. Of the former, the large stone circles at Stonehenge, Avebury and in other districts are examples, where tremendous stones were set up and capped by others of equal size, about which they probably performed their religious rites.

Of the burial chambers, the nearest to us is the Bride-stones at Congleton, where a long chamber of stone is divided by a slab, into which is cut a round hole giving access to the inner chamber. There is also a curved forecourt in front, and similar chambers have been found in Ireland, Anglesey, the Isle of Man and Western Scotland.

Most of these burial chambers had a passage and entrance - some later ones had false entrances, whilst in the forecourt the rites connected with the burial were performed.

Towards the end of the Neolithic period, about 2,000 B.C., a new type of material was introduced into the implements from travellers from the continent, who were gradually spreading themselves over Southern and Eastern England. This was a substance called bronze, which opened up new possibilities.

The art of bronze making spread slowly from the south and east. Because of the gradual infiltration of this art, the end of the Neolithic period saw stone and bronze used together before the dawn of the two Bronze Ages, the Early Bronze Age and the Middle Bronze Age.

Whilst bronze was introduced from the East, the centres in our island for the copper and tin needed were in Cornwall, Anglesey and in Ireland. It is to be expected that this new culture would have a great influence over the development of our district, partly because of its close proximity to Anglesey and Ireland, and also because there was a possibility of it being in communication by sea with Cornwall.

The early type of bronze axes were flat and rather similar in shape to the stone axes, and are of definite Irish origin. Axes have been found in our district at the Dog and Dart, Risley, Rixton, and at Winwick a knife dagger was discovered. Specimens of these Bronze Age tools can be seen in the Museum.

Probably, at that time Warrington was a major port of entry for these implements from Ireland, so now we have a sea route meeting the Neolithic crossing of the river here at Warrington, and the early site of our town assumes increasing importance.

These Early Bronze Age people were sometimes known as the Beaker Folk, from the squat, short-necked vessels they made. These beakers were often placed with their dead in burials of a similar nature to those of the Neolithic people, though the barrow or mound covering the burial chamber was round.

These new people did not oust the Neolithic race completely. They settled with them and merged their cultures and customs, but as they intermarried the later race pre-dominated.

We now pass to the Middle Bronze Age and see how our district has developed. So far it has only been a meeting place of routes and later a port of entry of traders from the west. Now we find that a settlement has taken place, and the first Warringtonians were inhabiting the district we know today. Before we see how this first Warrington had developed, let us look at the geographical setting.

The general configuration of the district would be similar to the one we see about us today, and as shown on a map of half-inch to one mile. To the south of the river would be the scarp of Hill Cliff and the Weston-Knutsford plateau, the average elevation being some two to three hundred feet, higher in parts, whilst north of the river, the fifty foot contour line would bend back from the river with the land rising to about one hundred feet. Through the wide valley thus formed between this high ground, the river meandered, joined by numerous streams.

There was no Ship Canal and no straight cutting along Chester Road. In all probability the actual course of the river would be difficult to define, as the land between the fifty foot contour line would be composed of peat marshes through which the river and streams wandered by diverse channels. Dense forests would cover the land up to the two hundred foot contour line, though woods on the more sandy type of soil would be less dense, and in these, pathways and small clearings could be made. Paths would lead down across the peat to the river crossing, where sailors from Ireland and elsewhere could land from their dug-out canoes. This would be the part where the river came nearest to the higher ground with only a narrow stretch of marshland, and in all probability would be at Walton. On the higher ground, fairly close to this crossing, would be the first settlement, probably at Grappenhall, where Euclid Avenue now stands.

In the Middle Bronze Age, the spears and axes of the earlier period had developed into a more complex design. Some of these axes have been found at Ackers Common, Latchford, and at Winwick, also at Runcorn, Wilmslow, Dutton and Frodsham, whilst axes of a later type were found at Ellesmere Port, Middlewich and Congleton.

Their pottery, too, was more highly developed, and in the urns they made they placed the ashes of their dead. These urns they buried under a mound, and these cairns or barrows have been found locally at Winwick, Croft and Grappenhall.

The discoveries of these urns and of others in Cheshire seem to suggest that settlement in our district, resulting from an infiltration from Ireland, Yorkshire and the Pennines, was continued from about 1500B.C. to 250B.C. As the urns found at Grappenhall cover a wide·range of various types, it seems probable that settlement there was practically continuous over a long period.

This place of settlement at Grappenhall was found by Mr Massey, and investigated in 1930 by Mr Leslie Armstrong, M.C., F.S.A., Colonel B. Fairclough, and the late Mr Dunlop, of the Museum. They found that an ancient burial mound existed. Fragments of bones were found, together with fragments of a cinerary urn. In December of the following year, Mr Massey discovered a pile of stones in his own garden under a mound of earth, and here a small urn was found. In 1933, when Euclid Avenue was being cut, further investigations were made by Mr Armstrong, Mr F. Dale and Mr D. Ridyard of the Museum. No more urns were found in this cairn, but from outside it fragments of a food vessel and a stone grain pounder were discovered. On excavating a portion outside the actual cairn, they found two large urns about one foot below the surface, each containing incinerated human remains, and numerous human remains buried in holes without an urn.

In 1934, further investigations on the first site yielded a cyst like grave four feet six inches long and eighteen inches wide, lined with stone slabs, though it contained no human remains. However, close beside the grave were found ashes and burnt bones which should probably have been placed in the grave. Other secondary burials were also found within the cairn at various points indicating that people of a later date made use of the same sacred site. In the grave, too, were flint arrow heads. Probably the settlers here were Neolithic people who had absorbed Bronze Age culture, and the fact that the food vessel is similar to many found in Ireland seems to indicate further evidence of infiltration from the west. The urn and food vessel from the site and three urns from nearby are in the Museum.

A barrow at Highfield Lane, Middleton, was discovered in 1859, and upon excavation, yielded a polished axe hammer, a bronze dagger and a cinerary urn. Mr May, speaking at a meeting of the Warrington Literary and Philosophical Society in 1894, mentioned a cinerary urn found in the sand near the Twenty Steps Bridge close to where Stockton Heath swing bridge is now.

Barrows found at Great Budworth, Delamere, Dunham Massey and elsewhere in Cheshire, indicate the settlement of the surrounding district at this time also.

Having thus established the first site of Warrington, let us see what type of life these first Warringtonians lived. The herding of such animals as the ox, pig, sheep and goat would continue from Neolithic times, and we have already noted the remains of ox bones discovered at Walton not far from the settlement. Some form of agriculture was also practised.

We have very little evidence of their type of dwellings, probably because they were constructed of wood and had very little stonework in them. Possibly they were round or rectangular in shape, similar to the wattle and

Sankey Street about 1900

daub huts made by the African natives today. Some authorities believe that the dead man's hut was burnt with him and the burial mound heaped over all. If such is the case, then the barrows would mark actual habitation sites.

The only dwelling discovered in Lancashire was at Bleasdale, near Fleetwood. Found under a barrow it was circular in shape with an open portico. Round it was built a large circle of palisades.

These Bronze Age people made ornaments in amber and gold, which they used as personal possessions. They spun thread and wove it into cloth, and probably towards the close of the period some form of wheeled vehicle was used, as wheels have been found near the sites of their dwellings in Yorkshire.

Their pottery was of improved design and decoration and, though carrying on the building traditions of the New Stone Age, they improved the hillsites and camps, and used the stone circles for religious rites. No doubt, as they settled more permanently on the land, and their personal possessions increased, the more talented individuals of the small communities, and those who had acquired greater wealth and more personal possessions than the majority, would become leaders or chieftains. Probably Warrington had its chieftains among the early settlers.

From about 750-100 B.C., a new wave of immigration from the continent spread to our district from the south and east, and also by sea via the west coast, bringing with it a new metal iron - which, however, by no means lessened the demand for bronze.

Two types of people came with this new culture. A more warlike people who built Hill Forts, and colonies of refugees who constructed the Lake Dwellings. The latter people were probably driven out of their homes by more virile tribes, and, settling down in this country, constructed their own peculiar type of dwellings.

Probably the community at Grappenhall existed for a while into this new period, as the discovery of the urn fields outside the actual original burial cairns points to an association with the earlier peoples of this new culture. Of what was their ultimate fate we have no evidence. They may have died out, or succumbed to a stronger race, or joined forces with them and retired to the protection of one or other of the nearby Hill Forts.

None of these forts are to be found in our own immediate district, but there are two sufficiently near to have influenced the development of the area during the early stages of the next influx of new culture, that of the Romans. Both are to be found in Cheshire, one at Helsby Hill and the other at Eddisbury Hill in Delamere Forest.

The first structure built on Eddisbury Hill was a palisade, probably a place of refuge constructed by the Bronze Age people, as a flat burial ground was found outside containing an urn. Then others, recognising the site for its defensive position and its commanding view of the Cheshire Plain, built the first rampart. This followed the natural contour of the hill, and consisted of a rampart, a ditch, and a lower bank on the outside of the ditch. It had a gateway and a guard chamber, and two entrances, south west and south east, the latter being approached by a sunken road. At the north west end, two ramparts and ditches were made, and also some attempt to carry the new outer line of defence round the old ramparts. A new entrance to the north was constructed later, and double span gates provided, whilst space for living accommodation was provided behind the ramparts. On these hearths were found several iron implements, and nearby an iron shoe to one of the gateposts. The Hill Fort on Helsby Hill was of a similar construction to the one we have just discussed.

The forts constructed by the Iron Age people indicate a higher level of culture ,and a stronger social sense, as the construction of such large works must have called for a combined effort.

Agriculture was more advanced on account of the introduction of a plough made of wood and drawn by two oxen. Herding of cattle would continue, but on a mixed farming basis. They would mine the rocks where metals were to be found and probably trade with the continent. They became Metallurgists, as is proved by finds of crucibles for smelting and moulds for casting iron implements.

Of the crafts, spinning and weaving were done, and much woodwork, even to the turning of shafts, while bones were worked into buttons, combs, needles and bracelets, and brooches and decorative ornaments of many types were made. They constructed chariots, and were adept at driving them, a fact to which their Roman conquerors paid tribute. If these wheeled vehicles were used, the ancient tracks joining various centres of population would be improved, in fact, those in the south exist today in the Icknield Way and the Berkshire Ridge Way.

The canoe and coracle would also become an added means of communication along the rivers as well as round the coasts, as they ventured further afield.

With regard to the second type of dwellings, namely Lake Dwellings, let us see what evidence exists for believing that a settlement of this type was made in our district.

When the Ship Canal was cut, and the lock joining it to the Mersey made at Walton, the two dugout canoes, now to be seen in the Museum, were found. The larger of the two canoes was found in the sandy silt close to the western end of the lock. During the excavations, innumerable piles were discovered in an irregular fashion for two hundred yards. They were about six inches thick and nine feet long, and were in two irregular lines, thirty feet apart. Between them were rows of stakes three inches thick and five feet long, crossed in herring bone fashion. At the eastern end, Mr May, who investigated, found oyster shells and bones ten feet from the surface, and sticks and sedges in horizontal layers. The canoe itself was found upside down, over eighteen feet below the surface, and twenty yards from the northern bank of the river. An anchor stone, eighteen inches square by nine inches thick, with a groove round it for a rope, was also found. Charcoal and signs of a hearth were observed. The second canoe was dredged from a depth of eighteen feet. All this evidence suggests a Pile Village Dwelling once existed at this spot.

Further evidence came to light more recently. A timber structure, supported on piles and resembling the early types of this kind of dwelling, was discovered at Howley. Owing to the fact that it was surrounded by buildings, no detailed examination was possible.

Whether the two canoes were used by the inhabitants of these dwellings is not known. Mention of them has already been made with regard to the Irish traders.

The pointed ends of the piles only reached to the same level as the canoe, which suggests the canoes might be older than the dwellings. On the other hand, their heavier weight might very probably have caused them to sink deeper and deeper into the soft marshy ground, which would no doubt be accentuated by the change in climate gradually taking place from warm dry to warm wet Atlantic type, and the Warrington settlement at that time would doubtless make an ideal retreat for refugees from the continent fleeing from war-like invaders.

Did the canoes, then, belong to some refugee adventurers searching for just such a retreat? Or were they left by traders from Ireland, or did they belong to the people of the Pile Village? Perhaps we shall never be sure, but the canoes are there in the Museum for all to see.

Very little is known of how the people of this age buried their dead. Probably they did so by cremation and inhumation. Of the later peoples, flat cemeteries have been discovered, whilst chariot burials have been found in Yorkshire.

With such settled communities placed up and down the country, it would naturally follow that those more powerful than their neighbours would gradually incorporate them in their social system. The chief of the stronger tribe would then elevate himself to the style and dignity of a prince. By the time the Romans cast envious eyes on our country, certain tribes had become attached to definite areas. Thus we have the Silures of South Wales, the Ordovices of Central Wales, the Deceangli of Flintshire, and the Brigantes of the Pennines. To which tribe our communities belonged, to those of Flintshire or the Pennines is not definitely known. Probably at various times to first one then the other, or they might have held out on their own until overthrown by the Romans.

Thus we have seen so far the gradual emergence of our district from the mists of the unknown, and in the next chapter we will follow its adventure a little further down the scale of History.

Chapter II
Roman Warrington

During the latter years of the Iron Age, the powerful state of Rome had extended her Empire into France, or Gaul, as they called it. Many fugitives from this conquest arrived at our shores. There did exist at that time a trade between that outpost of the Roman Empire and Britain. We probably exported slaves, corn, cattle, and copper and tin from Cornwall and Ireland.

The Romans had two good reasons for casting envious eyes on our island. First, from a military point of view it was harbouring enemies of Rome, and might therefore become a base of an attack by the fugitives from Gaul and their British allies in an effort to regain their lost lands. Secondly, it would be to the Romans' advantage for commercial reasons to hold the monopoly of the British trade, and develop it for themselves.

An attempt to conquer Britain was made by Julius Caesar, but had to be abandoned.

A Roman Soldier

However, in A.D. 42, the Emperor Claudius despatched a force of some forty thousand men, led by Aulus Plautius, against the kingdom of Cunobelin in the south-eastern part of Britain. Within the year, Colchester, the capital, had surrendered. Soon the Regni of West Sussex and the Iceni of East Anglia were conquered, and Aulus Plautius became the first Governor of Britain.

In A.D. 47, he was succeeded as Governor by Ostulius Scapula, who extended the Roman sway northwards by establishing a Roman station at Wroxeter near Shrewsbury, and launching an attack on the Deceangli tribes in Flintshire. He had to abandon this campaign, however, as his right flank became threatened by the powerful tribes of the Erigantes from the Pennines, and by attacks from the tribes in South Wales inspired by Caractacus, the son of Cunobelin who had fled thither on the defeat of his father's tribe in A.D. 43.

Scapula had therefore to turn his attention to the conquest of the great Hill-forts on the Welsh border belonging to the tribes of the Silures and the Ordovices. In this he succeeded, but Caractacus escaped and sought refuge with Cartamandua, the Queen of the Brigantes of the Pennines, whose capital was the great Hill-fort of Almondbury, near Huddersfield. But the Queen, to ensure the goodwill of her Roman neighbours, surrendered Caractacus to them, and, as we all know, he was taken captive to Rome.

In A.D. 69, after years of comparative peace, revolt sprang up amongst this same tribe, and Cartamandua was ousted. The Emperor Vespasian, realising that the tribe had thus flouted Roman authority and arms, and finding it was essential to secure this flank if they were going to succeed in their conquest of the Druids of Anglesey and the tribes of Wales, and eventually the tribes of Southern Scotland, appointed Petilius Cerialis in A.D. 71, to lead the campaign against the Pennine tribes.

New stations were established in Yorkshire, and the 9th Legion of Roman soldiers moved there from Lincoln. On the west, Chester (Deva) was established, and the 20th Roman region moved there from Wroxeter. Thus a "pincer-movement" was formed against the Brigantes. One by one the great Hill-forts were attacked and sacked. The excavations at Eddisbury have proved that it was deliberately destroyed after its conquest. Probably the same fate overtook the smaller fort at Helsby when Agricola, legate of the 20th legion, attacked Eddisbury.

In order to proceed further northwards, the invader would have to secure an easy crossing over the Mersey. We have seen that such a crossing existed at Warrington in the previous ages. Here the river was between tides, that is, twice in every twenty-four hours shallow enough to ford. It would be natural, then, for the Romans to have some form of camp or township at this place in order to keep open this way to the North. The original inhabitants of the pile-dwellings and the site at Grappenhall either succumbed to the invaders, if they offered any resistance at all, or were suffered to live on as slaves to the new Warringtonians.

Their choice of a site would be governed by the nature of the country. It should be on sufficiently high ground to be out of the reach of floods, yet near enough to control the passage across the ford. The actual site of the station was discovered in 1898 by Mr May, F.E.I., F.S.A. Scot., and was excavated by him during the succeeding years. We are indebted to Mr May's book, *Warrington's Roman Remains* for much of the account given in this chapter.

He found that the fortification and its adjoining suburb extended for nearly a quarter of a mile from the southern bank of the river at Wilderspool and into Stockton Heath. It was known to them as Veratinum. His most valuable excavations revealed many traces of the town.

Firstly, he discovered a great military highway running north and south under the fields to the west of the present London Road, Stockton Heath, now built over in part by Roman Road. This road has been traced at Winwick also, where its actual course can be traced in the fields near Alder Root Farm, and evidently formed the main route northwards to Wigan, Ribchester, on the Ribble, and ultimately to the Roman Wall across England.

Secondly, he found the foundations of a rampart originally of four sides, enclosing some three acres inside the field adjoining Messrs Greenall, Whitley & Co.'s Brewery in Greenall's Avenue. This rampart was surrounded by a ditch.

Thirdly, two fortified annexes abutting on to the west wall of the rampart were found.

Fourthly, foundations of dwellings and workshops were discovered inside and outside the fortifications. These workshops included two ore smelting and two iron refining furnaces in the Brewery field, and an iron smelting hearth in a sandpit nearby. Also eight or more glass-makers' furnaces, four bronze-smelting furnaces, and bronze-founders' and jewellers' workshops were found. Nearly fifty floors, hearths, ovens or furnaces for heating cauldrons made of clay were found for a quarter of a mile from the river on both sides of the highway towards Stockton Heath. In a private garden in Dundonald Avenue, Stockton Heath, three potter's kilns and traces of others were unearthed. Many smaller finds of pottery, coins, and objects in bronze and iron may be seen in the Museum.

From these discoveries, it will be seen that the Romans not only constructed a fortified camp or garrison station, but also an industrial town of no mean size.

As we have seen in the previous chapter, the Mersey was a port of entry or goods made from gold, copper and bronze, from Ireland, Wales, and the continent via the west coast sea route, and it is reasonable to believe that the Romans would carry on and extend this trade during their occupation. Flat-bottomed boats would be able to find their any up the river to this point, carrying their cargoes of metal so that it could be manufactured into various articles before being despatched overland by their network of roads to other parts of the country.

WILDERSPOOL ROAD

Wilderspool Causeway in the early 20th century

They worked the once famous copper mines at Parys Mountain, near Amlwch, in Anglesey, of which we shall hear more again later. At Great Orme's Head, Llandudno, they found and worked surface deposits of copper. In the Pennines they were busy extracting lead from the dales of both the northern and southern hills, especially at Middleton, Castleton and Youlgrave. Alderley Edge, in Cheshire on the way to these Midland mines, would not escape the Roman prospector's eye, and here, too, they found lead and copper. We can see, therefore, that their workshops at Veratinum were very near a plentiful supply of raw material.

Thus was the first actual town built here by the river akin in its industrialism to the town we know today. We shall find, too, that this industrial impetus given to it so long ago, rarely deserts our town through the succeeding ages, and we can proudly point to the fact that Warrington's industries have been useful to our national life since early times.

The first Roman finds were made when the Bridgewater Canal was cut in 1770. Again in 1787, Edward Greenall, whilst laying the foundations of Wilderspool House adjoining the Brewery, found a number of Roman articles. From 1801-3, when the Old Quay Canal was cut through Town Field, Mr Beamont questioned eleven men engaged on the work. From them he obtained clear evidence of Roman foundations, shafts, large quantities of pottery, and also that a road was cut through, and one witness stated that when the road was laid bare, "There seemed to be wheel tracks upon it made by vehicles not so wide as our own."

The actual exploration of the site, however, waited until Mr May commenced his excavations in 1898.

Two roads have been traced leading to the town. The more important one, coming from Northwich or Salinae, has been laid bare at various times. In 1800 this road was discovered running through a field called Street Lunt Back, pointing towards Hill Cliff. In 1831, Mr Beamont and Mr Robson found the same road in Town Field, and Mr Lyon of Appleton Hall, laid bare a section in Dogs Kennel Field in 1849. In Dogs Field, Stretton, it was found to be 18ft. wide.

Another road left the Roman station of Deva by North Gate, and skirting Helsby and Frodsham, came to Wilderspool much as the modern Chester to Warrington road does to-day. From Salinae, where the Romans worked salt, and from another station, Condate, lying just to the south of it, roads led to Chester, skirting the foot of Eddisbury Hill. All who passed that way would therefore see the devastation of that ancient Hill-fort, and realising the might of Rome, would know what to expect if they revolted against their conquerors.

All these roads are marked on the map, and indicate how the various routes focus on our town and river crossing. Let us now follow Mr May in a more detailed survey of the site and its finds.

The Rampart

This was discovered principally on the west side of the Brewery field on the western edge of the great road running into the town, as a continuous platform nine feet wide and one to two feet deep, though in Roman times it would be considerably higher. It was constructed of ashlar and rubble of local sandstone, faced on the outside with dressed stones and on the inner or road side with smaller stones. It must have extended along the north side of Greenall's Avenue, but most of the stones must have been removed, as only some twenty-four feet of it was found. Traces were seen, too, on the east side and on the south or canal side. Surrounding the rampart on the outside was a ditch, which must have been five feet wide and from three to five feet deep. There was also evidence of two gateways, one at the northern and the other at the southern end of the road in the form of square sandstone blocks with the socket holes in them for the pivot of the wooden gate. Fortified annexes were found on the outside of the western rampart.

Dwellings

The remains of a long corridor-house in two parallel walls were found at the north-west corner, with a stiff clay floor and low sandstone walls for supporting the wooden structure. Inside were found two hollow platforms of clay connected with fire holes and used as means of heating the building. These platforms were placed lengthways across the apartment, and were connected by flues seven inches in diameter underneath. The whole apartment was about 18ft. by 10ft.

32

Other buildings must have existed, both dwelling-houses and workshops, but as they were constructed of wood, no remains were found. Twenty or thirty clay floors probably mark the position of these huts or workshop sheds.

Furnaces

Of these, calcinating ovens, sow kiln floors, smelting and crucible furnaces, were uncovered at four different sites, and with them specimens of clay band and haematite ores, charcoal, coal, slag and iron in various stages of manufacture.

The most complete of these iron furnaces was found in the south-west corner of the Brewery field. Mr May describes it as a T-shaped furnace cavity enclosed in a platform of stiff bounder clay, 2ft. to 2ft. 6ins. thick, in the shape of two oblongs cojoined. In the middle of the larger was a circular hole 2ft. 4ins. in diameter and 3ft. 4ins. deep, with a fan-tail flue opening from it 4ft. 4ins. long. Leading off at right angles to the flue was a sloping trough or gutter for collecting the molten metal from the furnace pit. Other iron furnaces were also found in the rampart and also at the southern end of Roman Road, Stockton Heath.

Having obtained their metal from the ore, the workmen would have to refine it before it could be welded into useful forms. For this purpose, the hearth was a semi-circular platform of broken tiles and bricks built up to a height of five courses. In it was a circular pit lined with baked clay. From the base of this pit, a funnel ran down and out to the front of the hearth for running out the purified iron. From a detailed consideration of these and the other furnaces, Mr May concluded that the iron was worked in two ways.

The first method was to heat the ore with a charcoal fire in a pit with a blast from hand bellows introduced over the top and maintained until the metal was reduced, when it would be forged red hot without melting. The second method was to use two furnaces. Powdered ore was mixed with charcoal and blast introduced over the tog until the mass of ore melted. The slag would then be skimmed off and the crude or cast iron gathered at the bottom of the trough or ladled into moulds ready to be refined in a refining furnace.

Glass Furnaces

These glass furnaces are believed to be the only one of their kind so far found in Roman Britain. Local sand was used in the making of the glass as it was later by Robinson's Glass Works. Glass-makers' workshops were found at the southern end of the Roman town. Two others were discovered on the south-west part of the Brewery field between the walls of a fortified external annex. Smaller furnaces, used in making glass beads, were uncovered on the northern side of the rampart near the centre, again connected with the foundations of a workshop or building. Others were found outside the rampart in Roman Road, 80 yards or so from the Ship Canal. From the precincts of these furnaces, many specimens of glass, glass beads and slag were obtained.

Most authorities are agreed that with these small furnaces the Romans could make practically every variety of blown, pressed, crystal-coloured and cut glass. Specimens of their work found at Wilderspool can be seen in the Museum.

Pottery

Pottery ware forms one of the most easy means of dating and learning about a Roman camp-site. Fragments of pottery, being imperishable, are to be found on every site, and though many are unglazed, others are of the famed glazed or Samian Ware. This latter type indicates the degree of advancement in the arts of the period, and perhaps more important from the excavator's point of view, often has stamped on it the name or mark of the potter, and sometimes that of the owner too. Thus from knowing where and when these potters worked, one is given an indication of the date of the find spot.

Three potters kilns were found beneath the west side of Kimberley Avenue, a little north of its junction with Dundonald Avenue, a quarter of a mile south of the fortification. They consist of three furnace cavities, united at the back but separated in the front by two short piers supporting the roof. The encircling walls were of massive boulder clay, 3ins. to 9ins. thick, burnt to a depth of nearly an inch by the intense heat. In the hollow chamber behind, the fire from the three furnaces was concentrated, and the heat conveyed through the roof by two holes 2½ins. in diameter into the bee-hive shaped kiln built above it. The whole furnace measured 2ft. high, 5ft. wide, and 6ft. long.

A large amount of pottery was found near the kilns, much of it made locally. Mr May calls it Veratine Ware. It consists of large vessels for domestic use, vases, urns, and other vessels of good workmanship. The clay was shaped by hand first, before heating in the kilns. The commonest forms of vessels found were wide-mouthed urns with ring handles, triple vases, a small ornamented urn 4ins. to 6ins. high, and one large vase 14ins. high with three cordons dividing it into as many bands, and ornamented with a series of bosses. Others found were little pots 21 ins. high. at shallow dishes resembling hand lamps, cups supported by a stem and circular foot, large pans 9ins. high and l0ins. by 12ins. across the mouth, and jars and bottles with narrow necks and globular bodies.

Old Warrington Church

The names of the potters are stamped on the vessels, and were found to be native celts, not Romans, showing that the native population came to work for their conquerors. Whether these potters were descendants of the native Warringtonians living here before the Romans came, is not known. Four names are given by Mr May as being the probable potters of this town, and they are stamped on many fragments locally. The names are: ANIACO, ICOTASI, BRICOS, BRVCI.

Fragments of the Samian Ware were traced by the maker's name to come from extensive factories known to exist in Lezoux, Puy du dome district in France, Heilegenberg, near Strasburg, and Arezzo in Tuscany.

Jewellers Shops

These were found in the fortifications on the north side, and consisted of a central courtyard with a central water channel encircled by floors, furnaces and rubbish pits of the jewellers, bronze-founders and enamellers workshops.

Temple

Outside the fortifications, on the east side of Roman Road, Stockton Heath, was unearthed the head of a bronze figure of Minerva. As walls and platforms and a stone bust of the same goddess were subsequently discovered, also an altar-stone just outside the southern corner of the fortifications, it was thought that here had been erected a temple. It is known that Minerva, the symbol of wisdom, was the pationess of all the arts and crafts, and was worshipped especially by craftsmen, so what is more likely than the artisans of Veratinum should erect a shrine to her honour and worship her amidst their workshops here.

Thus we have a picture of the everyday life of the first Warrington township, a walled town or village with wooden dwellings for its workers and inhabitants, the majority of whom were probably native Celtic people. Down its main street would hurry the workers on their way to ply their trades, whilst soldiers from a cohort of the 20th Legion stationed at Chester, and who would be garrisoning the town, would lounge about the workshops, probably watching the local craftsmen fashion a new weapon, helmet, or piece of armour for them. Travellers and traders would be found here, doing business with the tradesmen whilst waiting for a passage across the river. Dominating the scene would be the long vista southwards along the Roman road.

As the Roman rule brought peace and security to the neighbourhood, later traders, not finding space to erect a workshop or home within the ramparts, would build outside, yet close to the road where passers-by could see them at their work, be attracted, and probably tempted into making a purchase.

Down by the river, boats from Ireland, Wales and elsewhere would arrive with the tide, and a busy scene present itself, as the smiths, jewellers and other tradesmen bargained for the cargo of raw material. There might have been a bridge of boats across the river here, too.

About the town, all would be bustle. The noise of the workshops, the noisy talk of the town and the clatter and smoke from the furnaces would be in complete contrast to the silence of the surrounding countryside, the marshes of the river, and the forested land to the north and south, cut through by the straight, solid Roman highway. Even today, the contrast is great, the noisy, smoky factories, and bustling streets, and southward, along almost the same road, the quiet lanes and green fields of Cheshire.

Chapter III
Saxon and Danish Warrington

The Roman occupation of this country is the only one of the various early occupations that can be fixed between two definite dates. They came, as we have seen, in A.D. 43. Then, consequent upon attacks by Barbarians upon Rome itself, the army of occupation left our shores in A.D. 410. Nevertheless, their mode of life and cultural influence remained for a considerable time until ousted by fresh invaders.

Naturally, now that the Roman military power was no longer in the country, contending factions of the original Celtic inhabitants sprang up, and a period of national anarchy prevailed. They quarrelled and fought among themselves to such an extent that there was no nationally organised resistance to the next group of invaders to our shores, namely the Saxons.

The Roman town at Wilderspool probably existed for a number of years after the Roman legions were withdrawn. There is no evidence to show the date of its final destruction. It may have been destroyed during the time of internal strife, when the Welsh-speaking Celts of the Firth of Clyde came down to war on the Irish-speaking Celts who had settled on the western seaboard and the Isle of Anglesey; or it may have survived these troubles and been destroyed during the wars between one or other of the seven Saxon kingdoms that the new invaders established in the country. One such likely episode we read of in the Saxon Chronicle. "In the year A.D. 607, Ethelfrith, the Saxon King of Northumbria, led an army to Chester and slew numberless Welshmen." As his route was from the north-east, he would doubtless pass through this district and, of course, being in the country of his enemies, he would sack and destroy any town through which he passed, either to or from Chester.

It must have been after the destruction of the Roman town that the present site on the north bank of the river was chosen. What caused the change we do not know, and can only conjecture that the builders of the new town held the original site in suspicion and refused to use it. Our district was then on the borders of two Saxon kingdoms, Northumbria and Mercia. As with all border districts, it must have been an eventful place in which to live, as it would at various times, come within the bounds of one or the other as their strength waxed and waned. Probably from this fact the lack of any definite evidence is due.

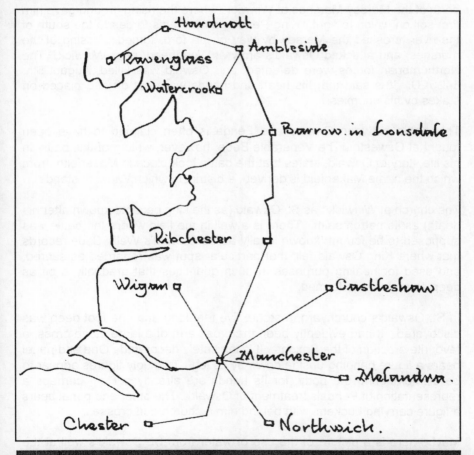

The Roman Occupation of Lancashire

We have already seen that one battle between the rivals was fought near to our district, now we find records of another. In A.D. 635, a young man named Oswald became King of Northumbria. He was a strong and wise ruler, and introduced Christianity to his people by inviting the monks from Iona to teach them. He extended once again the bounds of his kingdom to the Mersey, and was recognised as a leader and unchallenged king until King Penda of Mercia became jealous and challenged him to war.

Oswald gathered his army together on the South Lancashire plain to the north of the Mersey Marshes at Winwick, where the rising ground gave him firm soil on which to fight. King Penda gathered his forces to the south of the river, crossed the Mersey by way of the ford, forced crossing of the marshes, and attacked Oswald's army at Woodhead, near Winwick. The Northumbrian forces were defeated, and Oswald was killed, August 5th, 642 A.D. It is said that his head and hands were cut off and placed on stakes by his enemies.

This battle between Oswald and Fenda is often claimed to have been fought at Oswestry. The Venerable Bede, however, writing of this battle in his life story of Oswald, states that the battle took place in Maserfelth, from which the name Makerfield is derived, a district in which Winwick stands.

The church at Winwick has St. Oswald (as the king became known after his death) as its patron saint. There is a well in the field where the battle was supposed to be fought, known locally as St. Oswald's Well. Bede records that where King Oswald fell, that particular spot was regarded as sacred, and used for healing purposes in such quantities that gradually a pit as deep as a man was formed.

In St. Oswald's churchyard, a stone, five feet long and one foot deep was discovered. It had evidently been the cross arm of a large stone cross, a favourite erection of the Saxons. It is intricately decorated. One end panel bears a figure hanging upside down by its leg. Two ugly figures appear to be dismembering the body, for its hands are already cut off, perhaps a representation of Pendals treatment of Oswald. The other end panel bears a figure carrying buckets, with behind him a church and crosses.

Maybe here is a picture of the use of water from St. Oswald's well at the consecration of the church.

These crosses are practically all the traces the Saxons left. Some are just straight upright pillars decorated and inscribed, a fine set of which are to be seen at Sandbach in Cheshire. Later types have the cross arm introduced into them, and to one of these the segment at Winwick belongs.

Other traces of the Saxons in the district are found at Runcorn and Thelwall. The former was founded by Ethelfleda, the daughter of Alfred the Great. When the Danes coveted this well-situated estuary port, she built a castle, so that when the invasion came the inhabitants were able to give a good account of themselves.

Thelwall's association with the Saxons is well known to the people of Warrington from the inscription found on the wall of the Pickering Arms - "In 923 Edward the Elder founded a city here and celled it Thelwall."

For some years the Saxons had been forced to fight hard for the land they had conquered to prevent it falling into the hands of the new invaders - the Danes The Saxon Chronicle records many accounts of these struggles, which incidently, through these accounts, throws some light on Warrington and district in Saxon times.

In A.D. 894, the records show that the Danes arrived at a western city in the Wirral called Chester. "There the army (of Alfred) could not overtake them ere they arrived within the work. They beset the work some two days and took all the cattle thereabouts. They slew the men they could overtake without the work, and all the corn they either burned or their horses consumed."

In A.D. 913 the record runs - "This year, by the permission of God, went Ethelfleda, Lady of Mercia, with all the Mercians, to Tamworth, and built the fort there in the forepart of the summer, and before Lammas that at Stafford, and in the next year, in the beginning of the summer, that at Eddisbury. Then in the following year, after mid-winter, was built that at Chirbury, and that at Warburton and Runcorn."

In A.D. 923 the following is recorded: "This year went King Edward with an army, late in the harvest, to Thelwall, and ordered the borough to be repaired, inhabited and manned. And he ordered another army also from the population of Mercia, the while he sat there, to go to Manchester in

Northumbria to repair and man it."

Thus it seems that the Roman site of Warrington was no more, and that the ancient site of the hill fort at Eddisbury was in use again. What made these people .build their town on a fresh site? Was it the early Christians' aversion of a pagan place? Or was it that the Roman town was too near the river, and therefore subject to raids by attacking bands of Saxons, and later Danes, so that for security, the inhabitants moved further inland and higher up the valley?

Thelwall was evidently important enough for the king to order its rebuilding and defence. It was therefore probably the district's first line of defence with Runcorn against the new invaders. Perhaps marauding bands of freebooters were responsible for the reoccupation of the old site at Eddisbury behind the Frodsham hills and away from the shores of the river. This same river, up which their fathers had proudly sailed, was now a source of terror to them. Viking ships now came sailing up its wide estuary, bringing terror and death.

From the Doomsday Book, compiled by William the Conqueror, we have a picture of our district in Saxon times.

Of Grappenhall it records: "Osbem Fitz-Tesson owns Gropenhole and Edward of him. The same and Dot who were two free men held it as two manors. There is one hide and a half of virgate of land and rateable to the Gelt.... There are two serfs, one villein and three birdars. There is a wood one league long and forty perches broad. There are two bays (stands for deer)." In King Edward's time it was worth five shillings.

From this account we can draw a typical picture of Saxon village life. Edward and Dot would have a wattle hut in the woods. Hunting was their pleasure, and the deer would be driven into the bays and there speared or killed by dogs. The Gelt was the Government tax which they had to pay. Their serfs worked on the land, received their food but no wages and were liable to be sold. The villein was a little higher in rank than a serf, and held his land under the Thane of the Manor by right of some service rendered to his lord.

If he was sufficiently wealthy, the Lord of the Manor would possibly have his house enlarged to form a central hall, which from Saxon times to the reign of Queen Elizabeth, became the centre of family life.

In war, the sword, battleaxe and spear had become formidable weapons, whilst later they developed the bow and arrow. These sea-raiders, however, on acquiring land, settled down and became good husbandmen, eventually evolving a system of farming - that of open fields and common land which became the basis of English country life right down to the eighteenth century. Craftsmanship of many varied kinds developed in settled communities. The Venerable Bede mentions copper, silver and lead in his writings. Glassware was made, too, and candles formed the means of lighting the hall of the Lord of the Manor.

What of Edward's borough at Thelwall? This being a king's town, it would have a wooden stockade and a ditch surrounding it, and contain a large hall and numerous wattle cottages. Where exactly it stood we do not know, for no traces of it remain. Practically all that the Saxons have left us have been their stone crosses and their writings. The Romo-Britons were, of course, Christians before the Saxons came, and the new settlers, as we have already seen, were converted by the monks from Ireland, who had settled in Iona and come south at the invitation of Oswald.

The Saxon crosses now found up and down the country were probably preaching crosses, or may possibly have been erected to commemorate the conversion of some notable Saxon. The Sandbach crosses are believed to commemorate the conversion of Penda, King of Mercia, which according to Bede, took place in A.D. 653. Did this actually take place at Sandbach?

It took practically four hundred years from the recall of the Roman legions for our country to become a Saxon land, and hardly had that unity been achieved than it became subject to attacks from fresh invaders - the Danes and Norsemen. We have already seen how the Saxon Chronicle records the movement of the Saxon armies to meet the new menace, especially as far as our district is concerned. The first appearance of these invaders in 787 is recorded thus: "First came three ships of Northmen out of Haerethaland (Denmark), and then the reve (sheriff) rode out to the place and would have driven them to the King's town because he knew not who they were, and they there slew him."

From then onwards the raids increased, the number of ships taking part in them grew, and the places of attack became more widespread. Bede's church at Lindis was destroyed in 793.

We have already, at the beginning of this chapter, recorded the attacks on the west. Everyone knows of Alfred's struggle with the Danes and how they became settlers in the country. Sometimes the Danes and Norsemen worked together, at other times in opposition, joining with the Saxons against each other. It would seem that the Danes chose the lowlands of Eastern England for their settlements, while the majority of Norse settlements were in the north-western districts.

Under Alfred the Great, stiff resistance was put up against the invaders, but by 978 the Danes were in control and remained so until the Normans came in 1066. The Norse settlements in our district date from about 900 A.D., when Ingemund was compelled to evacuate Dublin by Irish forces. He and his followers crossed the Irish sea and obtained a settlement of land in the Wirral from Ethelfled of Mercia. It had its capital at Thingwall, and no doubt the influence of this Norse culture was felt here in the Mersey Valley. It has often been suggested that the suffix "ford" in a name is derived from the Norse "fiord," so that the names Latchford, Orford, etc., indicate most probably that the Norsemen were here.

Chapter IV.
Norman and Mediæval Warrington

In the last chapter, we saw how our district fared under the influx of Saxon, Dane and Norseman. Now we come to the period of the last invasion of our country by people from the continent.

It is well known how Norman William cast envious eyes on this country and eventually invaded it in 1066. Like all fresh invaders, the Normans brought with them a new mode of life that was to last, with very little change in its basic form, until the next threatened invasion in 1588, and in this chapter we follow the story of an individual family throughout this period. This is the first time that we can point to any one individual delinitely known to be living in our district. The story does not deal with the ordinary Warringtonian, but rather of the family into whose hands the land hereabouts passed with the Norman conquest, yet at times it gives us glimpses of the ordinary citizen and so builds up our picture of the town and its life in this period. For the material for our account we are indebted to that able citizen of Warrington, Mr William Beamont, whose book, *The Lords of Warrington,* may be found in the library.

By the time the Normans came, Warrington was the head of an Hundred, and as such is catalogued in William's Doomsday Book, in which he took stock of his new kingdom, and we cannot do better than start the story of this period with the Doomsday account of the town.

"In Walintune Hundred, King Edward held Walintune with three berewicks. To the same Manor there belonged 34 Drenghes who had that number of Manors in which there were 42 carucates of land and one hide and a half. St. Elfin held one carucate of land free of all custom except the Gelt. The whole Manor with the Hundred rendered to the King a farm rent of £15 less

45

2 shillings. There are now in the demesne two carucates, and eight men with one carucate. These men hold the land. Roger one carucate. Tetbald one and a half carucates, Warin one carucate, Radulf five carucates, William two hides and four carucates of land. Adelard one hide and half a carucate, and Osmund one carucate of land. The whole is worth £4 10s. Od. The demesne is worth £3 10s. Od.'

William found the northern part of his new kingdom a tough nut to crack. As a result of its stubbornness he laid waste much of the country, especially east of the Pennines. His conquest was helped forward by many sturdy land greedy warriors. To reward these he gave them part of his kingdom to further subdue, and from which they could carve out estates for themselves.

Reduced and impoverished as this part of the land was after the conquest, he nevertheless found in Roger of Poictou one who was willing to make his estate from it. Accordingly he bestowed the land between the Ribble and the Mersey upon him, on conditions of knightly service current in those times.

In order for him to hold these vast estates, and keep them in proper order, it was necessary, as it were, to sublet portions to others on similar terms to those on which he held the whole from the King.

On a brother Norman, Pagnus de Vilars, he bestowed the Manor and Hundred of Warrington. Mr Beamont concludes that Pagnus de Vilars held Warrington, with its three belewicks, or hamlets, of Little Sankey, Orford, and Howley in his demesne, and that he was also paramount lord of the remainder of the Hundred. He computed that the population at this time numbered not many more than 120, or 340 for the whole Hundred. The industrial activity of the Roman town had completely disappeared and the population was wholly dependent upon tilling and farming the land.

Once again the ford in the river becomes the controlling factor, and near to it, so that he had control of it, Pagnus de Vilars built his moated home and settled his retainers about him. One wonders here what Tetbald, Roger, Warin and the others thought of the times they lived in, when they saw a foreigner come into possession of their lands. No mention of them is made after the Doomsday Survey. Did they bow to the inevitable? Were they killed in opposing the conquest? or were they put into serfdom? We cannot tell.

This first Lord of Warrington probably died somewhere about 1156, leaving behind him seven children. The eldest, Matthew de Vilars, becoming the second baron. The records show little of him, except that his daughter, Beatrix de Vilars, succeeded her father as the third baron. She took as her husband one Richard Fitz Robert Pincerna, who thus, in the right of his wife, was the fourth baron. The Pincerna family took that name from the office of pincerna or butler, which they held under the Earls of Chester. Pincerna, as a name of office, appears to have been held in those times by a person of some consequence. From their office one can easily see how the name came to be changed into Le Boteler.

Richard, the fourth baron, was succeeded in 1176 by his son, William de Boteler,' and as his father had acquired the Vilars estates, his official connections with the Earl of Chester became less and he became more a Lancashire man.

During the reign of Henry II, in 1181, every person was called upon by his King to be ready to defend his country. Every man, therefore, between fifteen and sixty, was to have arms according to his rank. For this purpose William was to have a haulberk or shirt of mail, a breast plate, a sword, a knife and a horse. While each one of his retainers holding land over 40/- a year was to have a sword, a bow and arrows and a knife. Then in order that these arms might not rust through disuse they were to be shown twice a year to the officers of the franchise at a public gathering for that purpose.

The times were rough and warlike, and under the terms for the holding of his land William could be called on at any time to serve the King in war, or to help to pay for the same. So in 1196, when Richard I.'s war with France had left him with a depleted exchequer', William was called on to pay his share in the following way:--

"From William Pincerna, Knight, holding of the honour of Lancaster, twelve marks, to be excused crossing the sea with the third army into Normandy since the King's return from Germany, and for scutage on his fee, six marks."

47

William's activities, both local and national, were many. In 1208 he was summoned by the King to help repair and put into a state of seige the castle of Lancaster. We also find him accompanying the King's expedition to Ireland. About this time discontent and trouble was spreading in the land. Trouble which culminated in the great Charter of Liberties exacted from the King on Runnymeade in 1215. It would seem that William was a King's man, for he was not present at this assembly.

His castle stood secure on the Mote Hill at Warrington, and in between his national duties he enjoyed hunting, fowling and fishing rights in the forest of Burton Wood. Standing near to his house was the church of St. Elfin, a rough wooden structure, which had served well the people of the previous age. Now it had outlived its time, and William had a new one built at his own expense somewhere about 1226. Maybe it was his advancing years that caused him to do this pious act for the good of his soul, because seven years later the fifth baron of Warrington was carried to his grave.

The fifth Lord of Warrington left behind him two children, his eldest son, Almeric le Boteler, succeeding him as the sixth baron.

Since the Doomsday Survey was taken the population of the district had increased, and Mr Beamont computed that somewhere about 550 people lived here. There was no bridge over the river, no fairs, no real semblance of a town. The only building of any importance being the lord's hall on the Mote Hill, which would not only house his family but quite a considerable number of his retainers. Most of the population were farmers and soldiers when the lord called for their services in that way. About the hall bowyers, smiths, and armourers, would set up their booths. Amusements were restricted to the days when a church festival gathered the scattered population together, as at Christmas, when the Yule log was burnt, or at Whitsuntide, when the mumming plays were played in the hall. They also had the twice yearly weapontake, as laid down by Henry II. when each man showed his weapons and his skill in their use. A few of the people were freemen, the remainder viileins, to some of whom he may have granted a small plot of land to help to sustain them.

Almeric le Boteler died as a young man in 1235, and was followed by his baby son, William Fitz Almeric le Boteler. As the heir was under age, his wardship passed to the King, who sold it for £100 to William Earl of

Ferrars, as is shown by the following writ dated 4th September, in the nineteenth year of Henry III.

"The King to the Sheriff of Lincolnshire. Know ye that for a fine of £100 which Earl William de Ferrars hath paid us to have the wardship of the lands and heir of Almeric le Boteler until their full age and with their marriage, we command you to give the said Earl seisin of all lands of the said Almeric in your bailiwick."

The Botelers not only held Warrington but other estates elsewhere in the country.

One of the first things we find the new lord doing after he had reached mature years, was in 1255 to obtain from the king a charter for the holding of a three-day fair in his Manor of Warrington on the eve, the day, and the morrow·of the translation of St. Thomas the Martyr.

In all probability this saints day was one of those celebrated here and made the occasion of a gathering of the populace, at which it was natural for goods to be bought and sold. The fair thus may have been in existence before the charter, but had become of such importance that the Lord of the Manor saw in it the occasion of much profit to himself, and so took steps to legalise it and have it put under his control. For this privilege we have it recorded that William paid to the King half a mark in gold.

It is fair to conclude from this that the town was now fairly well established, and on account of its position on the ford had for those days a considerable traffic of travellers through it. Although the times were rough, the people had a deep religious feeling, which the Lords of Warrington quite often expressed in some gift to the church. So it is not surprising to find William Fitz Almeric le Boteler acquitting the monks of Whalley Abbey from payment of tolls within his Manor of Warrington.

In the following year, 1256, the King, Henry III., must have found his exchequer very low, for he commanded that all who held lands of the value of 15Li a year should become Knights and, of course, pay to him the fees demanded of such a rank. Amongst these was the Lord of Warrington, who thus became Sir William Fitz Almeric le Boteler.

The Town's growing importance can be seen from the fact that somewhere about this time Sir William had built the first bridge across the river. Between 1256 and 1259 a calamity occurred for Sir William, his house on the Mote Hill being burnt down. In the latter year he obtained from his feudal lord, lands in Burton Wood, where he built himself a new house - Bewsey Hall - which remained the seat of his family for long years to come. Also in. this same year a higher dignity awaited him, showing us his importance and standing in the county. The King made him the High Sheriff of Lancashire. "We command all our sheriffs of counties within which any part of our Honour of Lancaster is situate, that they neither hinder, nor in any wise suffer to be hindered in the keeping of the said Honour, William le Boteler, our keeper of the same."

A small charter granted in 1261 throws a ray of light on the ordinary man of the town. It tells us that one Jordan Fitz Robert de Hulton, either the Rector or late Rector of Warrington, granted to Roger de Hopton and his heirs the house that he had bought in the town for forty shillings from Sir William. It was signed by Henry de Tyldesly, the lord's steward or seneschal.

About this time, too, the Austin Hermit Friars established their Priory in the town, at Friars Gate, near the river and the bridge.

Warrington's entry in the Doomsday Book

Internal strife now began to show itself in the country. Simon de Montfort was in rebellion against the King. It appears that he was popular in the town. His arms were prominently placed in the Friary Church. Sir William fought under his banner. His death was much lamented locally and pilgrimages were made to the place where he fell. Sir William managed, however, to remain in the Royal favour, and in that of the King's son, Prince Edward.

So that when the Prince came to the throne Sir William was able to advance the prosperity of his town by obtaining from him a charter giving him the right to hold a weekly market on Fridays, and a yearly fair of eight days about St. Andrew's day. This charter was dated 5th November, 1277 and was granted from Rhuddlan Castle, where the King was preparing for his conquest of Wales. Some years later, in 1282-3, Edward demanded the presence of Sir William le Boteler on his campaign in Wales.

He issued his writ of assistance from Rhuddian commanding all bailiffs and others in the county to assist Sir William in raising a thousand strong men to serve in the war. In the accounts of the campaign we find the following entry: "To Master William le Boteler for the wages of one constable, two hundred and six archers, with captains of twenty, from Saturday, January 16, 1283, to Wednesday, January 27, for twelve days, £22 4s. Od."

Sir William's importance seems to have grown with his prosperity, for in 1287 he was summoned to a military council at Gloucester, and some years later, in 1291, to appear at Norham ready for military service against the Scots.

Wars were expensive, even in those days, and the King was again short of money. This time he issued writs to all landholders calling on them to show by what right they held their privileges, in the hopes of exacting fines from those who had usurped any franchise, or exceeded any charters they held. Sir William received one of these writs calling on him to prove before the King's Justices at Lancaster by what right he had fairs, right of warren, wreck of the sea and a gallows at his Manor of Warrington. These he was able to prove as holding by right of charters granted, and by long custom and usage in the case of the warren and the gallows. So he was acquitted without fine. Near the old Blue Coat School in Winwick Road there used to be a field called Gallows Croft, probably because Sir William's gallows was erected there for the execution of persons convicted of a capital offence in his Manor Court. This fact shows us how much the life of any town or village was dominated in those days by the Lord of the Manor.

Yet, although the Lord of the Manor held the life of his town in his hands, as it were, he sometimes, if he pressed his claims too far, found his tenants in open opposition to him. Such must have been the case in 1292 in Warrington, for in that year he and his tenants came before Sir Hugh Cressingham, the King's Justice, for a settlement of their dispute. The result was a charter of eleven points granted by Sir William to his free tenants of the town, giving them certain privileges. It proves to us that the people of the town were beginning to feel themselves as important as their master, and it gives us some small insight into the conditions under which the people of those days had to live.

First - He exempted his free tenants from tolls on articles bought or sold in his fairs or markets.

Second - He gave them the right to have their measures free. A right to use their own weights and measures when the law was silent as they had the right to use those laid down by the King. It had been stated in Magna Carta that one set of measures should be used throughout the kingdom, but no subsequent statute had ever laid down the concise amount. So for many years Warrington's butter pound had more than sixteen ounces, and a local bushel of wheat did not correspond to the imperial bushel.

Third - No damages should be made for trespass of the tenant's cattle, but according to the quantity of the trespass and by the judgment of lawful men of Warrington. Evidently Sir William had been extortionate in his demands upon any person whose cattle had trespassed on his private lands.

Fourth - They were to have the free right of feeding their hogs in all the lord's lands, except the woods around his house, and if they fed them in these woods they were to pay for the feeding.

These two privileges may seem strange to us, used to the fields and woods of to-day, but we must remember that in those days, no land was enclosed by hedges or fences, and therefore it was quite easy for cattle and pigs to stray on someone else's land were the swineherd to take his eyes off his charges for one moment. No doubt an avaricious landlord would be on the look-out for such happenings in order to extort his fee for trespass, and this would be the cause of numerous friction between neighbours.

Fifth - His tenants should not be put to take an oath against their will.

Sixth - If any of his tenants were placed at the mercy of their lord for a fault at his court, they could only be so put by a jury.

Seventh - Sir William declared he would not make any inquisition on his free tenants without the consent of the parties. This consent was probably given by the suitors at the lord's court or by the jury.

Eighth - The tenants should not be forced to keep any man taken or attacked by the bailiffs. People were often detained illegally in order to extort money from them.

Ninth - They should not be forced to drive away their own distresses. They did not intend that Sir William should transform them into his bailiffs and servants.

Tenth - They should not pay relief for their tenements, but according to the tenor of their grants. The granting of land was not always written down, but was often delivered verbally in the presence of witnesses. If a witness died it might have been difficult to prove the tenure, and any unscrupulous landlord could easily demand more than he was entitled to from his tenant if there was no witness to prove otherwise.

Eleventh - Sir William engaged that the keeper of the assize of bread and beer should be chosen by the free tenants themselves. The assize was the ordnance that determined the weight, measure, quantity, quality and price of these articles. Thus our ancestors secured the control of the assize to the court of the manor and the officers appointed by it.

From this charter it would appear that Sir William had, before he granted it, not been so very fair in his dealings with his tenants, or otherwise they would not have demanded these rights and privileges. The tenants must have grown in numbers and to have increased in importance in the life of the town in order thus to have stood up for their rights against their lord.

Sir William was now taking an increasing part in the national life, and with these affairs and those of his estate he must have been a very busy man.

In 1294 he was summoned to meet the King to discuss urgent national affairs consequent upon the war with France. In the following year he was again called upon to attend Parliament at Westminster as a peer of Parliament. Sir William's Manorial Court was a place where suits were tried and important business transacted from all over his fee. Many of his tenants, like the Lords of Culcheth, Sankey or Penketh, were required to send two beadles or bailiffs to the court and who were there sworn to serve the lord's processes in their respective districts, and were to proclaim the assize of bread and beer when the court had fixed it. Sir William now allowed these others to send only one bailiff to his court.

In 1301 we again find the Lord of Warrington on active service, for in that year he was summoned by the King to appear with horse and arms at Berwick ready for military service against the Scots. Two years later he was again with the King in Scotland. Some few years later, however, he died. He had lived beyond his three-score and ten, a ripe old age considering the campaigns in which he had been engaged, and his journeys about the country on his own and the King's affairs. His life had been a full one. He had advanced his own prosperity, and with it that of his town, in securing for it the markets and fairs. He had established a Friary, rebuilt the Parish Church and put himself on amicable footings with the tenants of the town, and had their welfare and that of the town at heart. He had three sons and two daughters. His eldest son, Henry, died during Sir William's lifetime, so he was succeeded by his grandson. Sir William Fitz Henry le Boteler, as the 8th Lord of Warrington in 1304.

One of the first charters granted by the new lord makes the first mention of the bridge and Friary and his concern for the cleanliness of the town. We give the charter in full. *"William Le Boteler, Lord of Werinton, granted to William de Hereford a place of land lying between the house of Lawrence the baker and the bridge of the Merse at Werinton, and also granted him a place of land in Alderswell, lying near the ditch of the friars of Saint Augustine, except that the said William de Hereford or his heirs were not to place any dung or filth upon the highway or anywhere else but on their own land or outside the town. They were to pay 5/- rent, to grind all their grain and malt at William Le Botelers mills at Werinton and Sankey and were also to do foreign service."*

To others he also granted land about the same time. One of them being his own park keeper, to whom he allowed five acres in Burtonwood for twelve years at 5/- a year - a rent of 1/- an acre.

Like his grandfather, he was summoned to assist the King in his wars in Scotland in 1309.

In the following year Edward II granted Sir William the right to collect tolls from the bridge at Warrington. We will only give here a selection of the items on which the toll was to be paid. The full list can be found in Mr Beamont's Lords of Warrington, Vol. 1, p. 136-9.

For every		
	horse, mare, cow	½d.
	ten sheep	1d.
	dozen Lampleys	¼d.
	1,000 herrings	1d.
	weigh of cheese and butter	¼d.
	tun of wine or cyder	½d.
	cartload of honey	1d.
	piece of cloth	1½d.
	hundred pelts of sheep, goats, stags, hinds. deer, does, hares, rabbits, foxes, cats and squirrels	½d.
	cartload of canvas	3d.
	sack of wool	½d.
	cartload of wood	½d.
	coals	½d.
	1 cwt. of brass, tin, copper	2d.
	cartload of iron or lead	1d.
	ship coming to the town with merchandise	3d.

From this short list we can see that the fairs and markets of our town attracted the best of everything produced in those days.

The bridge must have presented a lively scene on the days preceding a fair, as the travelling packmen and merchants lined up to have their baggage examined and to pay the toll required. Doubtless a few brawls were witnesed as some unscrupulous merchant was caught in the act of hiding some tasty article in the hope that he would avoid the toll. But we can be sure that the keen eyes of the man appointed by Sir William to collect the toll would be on the watch for such occasions, which, if of a serious nature, would probably end in the Manorial court.

In 1314 Sir William was again summoned to Berwick to help repel the Scots. Whether he was present at Bannockburn in the same year we do not know. Seven years later, we find Sir William again concerned for the outward appearance of his town, for he obtained letters patent from Edward II at York which "Empowered his beloved and faithful William Le Boteler, Lord of Warrington, towards paving of the town, to collect for the next five years tolls on all articles brought into the town for sale." Thus our town had paved roads before many of its neighbours.

The following year found the Lord of Warrington summoned once again to help the King quell a rising of the Scots. He was to prepare with all haste, with horse and arms to Newcastle. It would appear that the population of the district was growing steadily about this time, for Mr Beamont records many instances of land being let to various people at rentals ranging from 1/'- to 1/6 an acre, and always with the proviso that the tenant should grind his corn and malt at his lord's mill.

The eighth baron lived till 1330, and then was succeeded by his eldest son. Sir William Fitz William Le Boteler, who became the ninth baron. The town was growing apace and taking on the semblance of the plan we know today. Streets were being formed, and Sir William granted two plots of land to "One Matthew de Southworth in Market Strete."

At this time the lord seemed much concerned with his lands and estates at Burtonwood, for we find him leasing large parts of it to tenants subject to them burning and clearing the woods and bringing the land under cultivation, and so to improve his lands. He was concerned also with the rights of many of his tenants for use of the common lands, and had occasion in many instances to restrict the use of these lands except those they held according to their leases. Probably many of them quietly added to the numbers of cattle and pigs which they kept on the common lands, and Sir William, desirous of keeping the land in case he wished to enclose it at any time, was keenly determined to keep them within bounds.

Burtonwood was fast becoming an outlet for the surplus population of the town. Cultivation gradually enclosed on the woods, though some three hundred acres of wood still remained of what previously must have been an extensively wooded area.

National affairs claimed the attention of the ninth baron just as with his ancestors, and we find him one of the King's army in garrison on the Scottish borders, and probably he later accompanied the King in his campaigns in France, and it is possible he was with the Black Prince's army at Poitiers.

In 1363, William, son of Robert le Bakester, was granted a piece of land in the town near the Market Gate between the tenement of Adam de Lever and the great house formerly held by Matthew de Sotheworth. The tenant was also allowed to trade in bread, iron, fish, and other saleable articles and also to sell without toll. The ninth baron was 71 when he died, and his life appears to have been as busy as his grandfather's was before him. He had spent a large part of his time in the King's service abroad and in Scotland, and whilst at home had looked well after his estates. He secured another paving charter for his town, which he could see was steadily increasing. He caused the Parish Church to be rebuilt and enlarged, and assisted the Friars by making them a grant of land.

Old Warrington Market Place

His eldest son predeceased him, so he was succeeded by his second son John, who was 52 when he became the tenth baron. He had accompanied his father to the wars and also managed the estates for a number of years before his father's death. He was probably the only one of his family to be experienced in the administration of affairs when he inherited the title in 1380. Whilst managing the estates for his father, Sir John, with other local gentlemen, helped to rebuild the bridge across the Mersey, as the previous bridge had been swept away about 1364. The new bridge was completed in 1369.

We have already made mention of Market Gate. Now we find Sir John buying from John Perusson, the smith of the town, all his messuages which were formerly belonging to William Payne in Sankey Street and upon Stanfield. In granting land or houses to anyone in the town, Sir John made it a condition that the grantee should not deposit filth of any kind upon the public highway.

Sir John continued his interest in national affairs and was frequently called to the King's Parliament. When Richard II sailed to Ireland in 1394, Sir John, with nine others, were made justices's of the peace for Lancashire in the absence of the King. Two years later he was expressly commanded to apprehend all persons found to be outlaws. In 1397 he was again one of the country's representatives in Parliament, and for his services he received xvili. and viii. shillings, about four shillings a day.

While the King was in Ireland, Henry Bolingbroke, Duke of Hereford, who had been dismissed abroad, returned to England in 1399 to regain his estates; and later the crown. He landed in Yorkshire, and summoned his friends to his aid. As Bolingbroke was the son of Sir John's feudal lord, the Duke of Lancaster, the faithful Sir John marched to his aid, but died on the way at the age of 72.

Like his grandfather, he had spent his life in national and local service, had been ever careful of the cleanliness and growth of his town and estates, and mindful of his religious obligations, had built the Boteler Chantry in the Parish Church. Abroad, he served in the wars in France, and was made a prisoner by the Moors of Africa when accompanying the Duke of Lancaster to that Court, and was only finally released from prison on payment of a handsome ransom.

He left behind his wife, two sons and three daughters, and his eldest son William succeeded to the barony.

Henry Bolingbroke, on regaining his estates and the crown, created William a Knight of the Order of the Bath in honour of his father's faithful service. On the day of the Coronation, Sir William was in the procession as one of the six Dukes, six Earls, and nine hundred Knights who accompanied the King on that day.

In the sixth year of the King's reign, certain nobles in rebellion had been defeated at Shrewsbury. The King ordered Sir Robert Legh of Adlington to meet the Prince of Wales with one hundred bowmen at Warrington in 1405 The Prince probably stayed at Bewsey Hall. What excitement there would be in the town, the sables, purples and coats of arms displayed by the knights and swaggering men-at-arms and bowmen dressed in the livery of their masters, parading or lounging about the town, and still greater excitement when the Prince arrived, and later departed to join the King at Pomfret.

About this time, Sir William granted permission to Sir William Daas, parson of Winwick, to build a weir in Sankey Brook to catch fish. It is difficult for us to realise that the Mersey and its tributaries were then clear running streams full of fish of many varieties, and a source of food supply to anyone who held fishing rights from the Lord of the Manor.

Henry V, like many kings of England before him, believed he had the right to the throne of France, and accordingly in 1415, collected an army together.

On April 5th of that year, Sir William indentured with the King to attend him to the war for a year with ten men at arms, and thirty archers, at a wage of 2/- a day for himself and 1/- a day for the men at arms and 6d. a day for each archer. He also contracted with the Sheriff of Lancashire to bring a further 50 archers to serve. Sir William, with his retinue, joined the assembling army at Southampton and sailed to France. Landing at Harfleur they besieged the town and captured it. But for Sir William this was a tragic journey, as he contracted the Plague and died. His body was brought home and laid to rest in the Friary in a marble tomb.

His son John only lived a few years, and on his death at the age of 28, it was discovered he held estates in Wiltshire, Essex, Bedfordshire, Nottinghamshire, Warwickshire and at Bispham in Lancashire, as well as the Manor of Bewsey with extensive lands in Burtonwood and the greater part of the Manor of Warrington.

These vast possessions, however, were tempting to other gallants in those days, some seeking to enrich themselves by forcibly carrying away rich girls or widows and forcing them into marriage. On the death of her husband, the lady Boteler cared for her children in the moated house at Bewsey. Five years later, however, a William Pule forcibly entered the Hall and carried her away to Birkenhead, where at Bidston Church he forced her to marry him, taking her into Wales and eventually bringing her back to Birkenhead where she was rescued by Sir Thomas Stanley. She sent two petitions to Parliament, both of which were granted, one, that her abductor be accused of treason and also that he might be prosecuted in Lancashire, in spite of the offence being committed in Cheshire. Whether Pule was ever apprehended, records so far have not shown.

The twelfth baron was followed by his son John, who was knighted in 1448. As he was a young boy when his father died, others were appointed as guardians of the estates, and as a result, they must have been sadly neglected, for in the year he was knighted, the young baron obtained a grant of £100 from the King for the repair of his estates. In 1453 he persuaded the Archbishop of York to issue letters granting all Christian people their indulgence if they contributed something towards the repair of the bridge at Warrington.

This bridge stood practically on the present site, and was approached by a street called New Street. At one end, one of the local Friars begged for alms. New Street, now Bridge Street, would be very narrow and lined with wooden houses with overhanging stories above. Shops were without windows, with a form of pent-house overhead. Passage along New Street on crowded market days must have been akin to the narrow end of Sankey Street to-day on a Saturday evening.

The thirteenth baron was only forty when he died. He was buried in the Parish Church, where the figure on his tomb depicts him dressed in plate armour with a shirt of mail and sword and dagger. He had been married three times and left eight children. His eldest son, William, succeeded him as Lord of Warrington. Of how Sir John died there seems some doubt, but an old manuscript, quoted by Mr Beamont, tells that he was murdered by Lord Stanley's procurement.

His son died in 1471, probably as a result of wounds received in the battle of Tewkesbury in the Wars of the Roses which was raging at that time. He was just 21 when he died, and, having no children, his brother Thomas succeeded him. Thomas was summoned to London to receive a knighthood, but family papers speak of him without the prefix "Sir," so he probably declined the honor. The misrule of King Richard led to the Field of Bosworth, where Thomas Boteler, being a Lancastrian, must have been present, and was knighted either on the field of battle or soon afterwards. He was later at the battle of Stokefield when Lambert Simnel challenged the King's forces, and his loyalty to the King was rewarded by his being made Justice of the Peace for the county in 1488.

Two years later, at Bewsey Hall on January 5th, Sir Thomas sat in his hall to receive homage of some of his tenants and feudal retainers. The Lieutenant Justice of Chester and many of the local gentry were present, and Sir Thomas' steward, Henry Doker, was the master of ceremonies. Here came Randle Sankey to pay 10/- and do homage for the lands he held in Little Sankey. Also came Hugh del Bruche, doing homage for lands he held under the Lord of Warrington in Sankey and Orford. Then followed three others, tenants, who paid their reliefs but did no homage as the lands they held were not under the knight's service.

The year 1495 must have been a red-letter day for Sir Thomas and the people of Warrington, for in that year the King and his Queen came to visit the Countess of Richmond, his, mother, and her husband the Earl of Derby, at Lathom House. In honour of the occasion, the Earl had a new bridge built at Warrington, which the King and his retinue were the first to cross. Sir Thomas, accompanied by his Rector, Sir Richard Delves, and by the Prior of the Friary, Sir Richard Browne, and accompanied by a goodly company of local gentlemen, and surrounded by a crowd of the town's inhabitants, welcomed the Royal party. What a pageant of colour there would be! The King's hundred footmen in royal livery, the colourful liveries of the local gentry present, the gay banners hanging from the houses, and the music and happy noise of the gathered populace, would all combine to make a memorable day. After their stay at Lathom House the royal party spent a night at Warrington, either with Sir Thomas or with the Rector, before going on to Manchester.

On one occasion it is recorded that a ceremony for payment of reliefs was held in the Friary at Warrington, when Robert Fitz-William Blundell came to do homage. Lately come of age, he would appear before Sir Thomas clad in armour, and would repeat aloud after the master of ceremonies the following words: "Know ye Sir Thomas Boteler, Knight, my liege lord, that I, Robert son of William Blundell, do become your man from this day forward to the end of my days for life and, members and worldly honour, and unto you I will be faithful, and will bear true faith for the lands I hold of you, saving only the faith I owe to my sovereign lord King Henry."

During this period of domestic activities, the Manor House at Bewsey was extended. The old house of wood and plaster had contained a hall with a turret, a room for the private use of the family, a private chapel, buttery, pantry, kitchen and cellars and sleeping chambers. To these were added a great chamber or gallery, four smaller chambers and additional kitchens, all built of brick and contained within the bounds of the moat.

In 1505, Sir Thomas took on another duty, that of Royal Chief Forester of Toxteth forests and chases, and stewardship of Liverpool, which in those days was not a port, Chester and Parkgate being ports.

The previous year, Lord Stanley, the first Earl of Derby, and builder of the bridge, died, leaving two sums of money, one to free the bridge from tolls, and the other to keep it in repair. It appears that while the crossing of the river was by ford, the Boydels, lords of the Latchford Manor, then a separate township, had the right to collect the tolls for the crossing, the approaches to the ford being through their enclosed lands. Whether they claimed tolls from the bridges built by the Botelers is not known, but in 1504 they claimed the fee for freeing the bridge for tolls, a claim which Sir Thomas disputed. The result of the settlement of these rival claims is lost, but the bridge became a free thoroughfare. This step would considerably affect the prosperity of the town, as it would dispense with the weekly market and yearly fair which the Boydels had secured for their Latchford township, and so allowed the people to attend markets and fairs in Warrington without having to pay toll.

In 1509, Henry VII died, and his son ascended the throne, and four years later invaded France. This opportunity the Scots used to invade England, but the people of the North rose to repel the invader, and so we find Sir Thomas fighting in the King's cause at Flodden Field, The majority of local knights and gentlemen fought under the banners of Lancashire and Cheshire, whilst even the Abbot of Vale Royal led a goodly company, and Sir Thomas' chaplain, Sir William Plumtre, went with him.

After this exciting episode, Sir Thomas lived quietly at home, discharging his duties to his estate, acting as Justice of the Peace and arbitrator in his friends' and neighbours' quarrels. Early in 1522, as though foreseeing his approaching death, he made his will, which, after providing for the needs of his family, set aside 500mks, and certain lands in his possession to be used to found a Grammar School in the town, and also that his body be laid to rest in the Boteler chapel in the Parish Church.

During the time of Sir Thomas' son, Thomas, we find the Manor court sitting frequently to try people who had trespassed on another's land or assaulted or inflicted wounds on other persons. Fines were imposed for disobeying the lord's officers, stalling the market, laying filth on the streets, selling goods of inferior weight or quality and other such offences. "Burleymen" were appointed who assessed damage for trespass, and sworn in at the court were the lord's constables and other officers. As these meetings coincided with the fairs, cock-fighting and bear-baiting would be carried on for amusement.

In 1526, carrying out the wishes of his father, Sir Thomas, his son established the Grammar School, and set aside a house in Back Lane (now School Lane) for the use of the schoolmaster. Thus was established the Warrington Grammar School.

On the occasion of the King's marriage to Anne Boleyn, Thomas Boteler was knighted, thus becoming the second Sir Thomas, and the following year was appointed High Sheriff of Lancashire. These were the days of religious unrest, when the King and his subjects looked with envious eyes on the abbeys and monasteries, and the Friary at Warrington was not allowed to escape destruction. The Prior and brethren were driven from their home, and the building passed to the King, who sold it to one Thomas Holcroft in 1540. This man evidently seized the opportunity the times offered, for he bought other religious property and land, including the Abbey of Vale Royal. Though the Friary was destroyed, the chapel attached to it was secured for the use of the local inhabitants for years to come.

When a new parson entered a living, the Pope claimed the first year's profit and one-tenth for every year afterwards. In 1291, when it was first claimed, the Warrington Vicarage was rated at £13 6s. 8d., and £1 6s. 8d. for the ·tenths; in 1534 it was increased to £40 and £4, and was now payable to the King, as he had assumed the position of Head of the Church.

In 1550 Sir Thomas died, and was succeeded by his son, also Sir Thomas, who became the 17th baron. In 1563 he contracted with Sir Richard Brooke, of Norton, for their children to marry, and in the contract is given a list of property held by the Botelers in the town, and it shows once again that trade was increasing. An old chronicler records that the inns of the time were well furnished, and accommodation for travellers very good. One of the travellers, Leland, who appears to have journeyed all over the country wrote of the town, "It is a paved town and has a better market than Manchester."

Edward, Sir Thomas' son, for whom he made the contract, never married the daughter of Sir Richard Brooke, indeed, he appeared to be a peculiar person, for even before his father's death he sold his rights to the estate. His father, however, more mindful of the family honour, recovered them, and realising the nature of his son, left a deed when he died, leaving the estates to his daughter. On her father's death, she immediately transferred them to her brother Edward who, in return for money, stripped himself of his estates, so that with his death the Boteler family as Lords of Warrington ceased.

Thus in five hundred years since Norman William bestowed the Manor on his retainer, we have seen eighteen or more generations of the same family in control of the Manor. We have seen the town established on its present site because, in the first place, the Lord of the Manor chose it for his home, and settled his servants around him. During these years the family were practically dictators of the life of the town, and in at least four out of the five hundred years, the common people were their serfs.

Because of its importance on the chief crossing of the river, the town grew in significance, and the Boteler family sought to add to this by obtaining markets and fairs, bridging the river, granting charters, paving the streets and seeing they kept clean and neat. Warrington commenced the period as a village, and by the close of Elizabeth's reign had become a town of consequence.

Diligent as the family were for the affairs of their manor, they were none the less diligent in the affairs of the nation. They sat on the seat of national council, acted as the King's deputy and justice in the county, and when necessary buckled on their armour to fight for their country or the King's cause.

Many of the lord's servants became free men and owners of land and property in the town and district, some as farmers, others as merchants, for as the fairs and markets attracted more people and the village grew from a scattering of houses to a system of streets, merchants began to arrive and

The Plague House in Wash Lane, Latchford, dating from 1650

industry settle there. About its narrow streets, under the overhanging gables, smiths, millers, shopkeepers, cowled fliars and makers of weapons hurried or idled, the travelling merchants contested the right of way with local farmers intent on similar business, the motley throng giving preference to the gay cavalcade of the lord of the manor or other local gentry.

The surrounding villages of Latchford, Orford, Sankey and Burtonwood, though not yet part of the town, were linked with its life as most of their lands were held under service to the Botelers.

The town was now settled on its site, and gradually gathered, as we shall see, the industrial impetus which has carried it to the present day.

Chapter V
The 17th Century In Warrington

In the last chapter we followed the family fortunes of the Lords of Warrington, as during those five hundred years, the prosperity, destiny and fortunes of the inhabitants of a town was bound up with the fortunes of the great land-owners, and they were at the mercy of their lords' whims and fancies.

More especially was this so at the beginning of the period, when settlements were small and mostly composed of the lord's retainers. By the time of the Tudor period when our last chapter closed, these settlements had grown into towns, and the nucleus of the lord's servants was swamped under an influx of tradesmen, craftsmen, merchants and lesser landowners, with the result that while the lord of the manor was still paramount, acting through his manorial court, the new burgesses began to develop a co-operative life of their own, demanding and obtaining more and more say in the government of their lives.

The arable land of the town was still farmed on the open field system, a number of strips in each meadow land often allocated to each farm and the right of pasturage on the common land and in the arable fields after harvest granted· also. The lord, however, kept control over his own mills, and made it a condition, as the Botelers did, that corn should be ground in his mills.

The co-operative life of the town found expression at the annual fairs, the Saints' days and at such times as Easter, Christmas and May Day, local mumming plays at these times giving place to shows given by bands of strolling-players in the local inn yard. May Day was a public holiday, the men and women rising early to go a-maying in the woods, returning with flowers and garlands with which to decorate their homes, and to deck the Maypole, around which the festivities for the rest of the day were carried out.

Very often near the Maypole was the town's stocks and pillory. We are all familiar with the stocks at Grappenhall and Lymm, while the Latchford stocks can be seen in the Museum. The stocks were in charge of the town's constable, elected by the Manor court. It was the constable who prevented assaults and bloodsheds and unlawful assemblies, executed warrants and arrested suspected persons and confined them till the next meeting of the court and then carried out the punishment decreed to be inflicted on them.

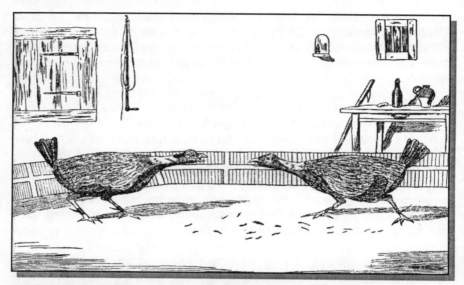

Cock fighting, which was once popular in Warrington

Cock fighting, bear baiting and hunting were the sports enjoyed. Cock fighting pits are still in existence in the grounds of Lymm Hall. Particularly addicted to this sport was the last Lord of Warrington, who often attended mains at Winwick and Lymm.

Gone were the wooden huts of the early Normans. Buildings in wood and plaster, the familiar black-and-white, lined the streets of our town, streets which were for the most part paved.

With the passing of the last Lord of Warrington and the mergence of the Boteler estates into those of Edward Boteler's cousin, the Earl of Leicester, we will leave the fortunes of that family and confine ourselves to the story of the town itself during the succeeding years.

England under Elizabeth has often been called Merry England, though in 1588 tidings of Philip's threatened invasion swept the land. Anxious eyes in the streets and the surrounding district looked towards the distant hills, and saw the beacon fires blazing and telling of the approach of the Armada. The fire on Mow Cop by Congleton passed the news on to Rivington Pike, Hill Cliff to Frodsham. Helsby to Beeston and on to Chester. Around the night sky they twinkled, and good men saw to their arms. Then what rejoicings when the tidings came of the enemy's defeat, and the people echoed the words of their Queen, "God blew with his winds and they were scattered."

Following the defeat of the Armada, the town settled down to a normal life of increasing trade and gradual expansion of its boundaries.

Few records of the town exist during the closing years of the Tudor dynasty or the times of James I. When his son came to the throne, however, troublesome times were brought to the country, which resulted in the Civil War, which broke out in 1642. During this period, the geographical position of our town forces it to play no mean part in succeeding events.

Warrington was thought to be conveniently central for the loyal counties of Lancashire, Cheshire, Shropshire and the North Midlands to rally to the Royal standard, and for this purpose the Earl of Derby came to raise troops, but taking advantage of his absence from the council, others suspecting his loyalty, persuaded the King to set up his standard at Nottingham.

The Earl of Derby, however, remained at Warrington collecting his forces, and by September he had some 4,000 foot soldiers, 200 dragoons, 100 horsemen and 7 pieces of ordnance. With these he moved to attack Manchester, but being unable to take the city, sent his army south to Shrewsbury to join the army there, while he remained at Warrington to gather fresh men, during which time his first army fought with the King at Edgehill.

Lord Derby remained in garrison here during the latter-part of 1642 and the early months of 1643, except for leading attacks on Bolton, Blackburn and Preston.

A statue of Charles I

Dr. Ormerod, in his *Civil War tracts of Lancashire*, quotes the following letter written by one James Jesland, of Atherton, to his friend, Rev. Divine, in London, in December, 1642, which gives us an insight into conditions then. "The Lord Strange, now Earl of Derby, is the great ringleader of the Popish faction and Malignant party and keeps his rendezvous at Warrington, whither great multitudes of ill-affected people both of Lancashire and Cheshire doe daily resort, it lying on the frontiers of both. They make daily great spoil in the country, which hath now awakened and so incensed them, that they are, tide death, tide life, resolved to endure it no longer."

A parliamentarian pamphlet, printed in Dr. Ormerod's *History of Cheshire*, describes one of these sorties by the Earl's forces upon Mr Brooke's house at Norton. It describes how Mr Brooke had only 80 men in the house, and how the Royalists attacked with cannon. Their shooting could not have been very accurate, for one of Mr Brooke's men stood on the tower shouting, "Wide my hand on the right, now wide on the left," till "he made them swell with anger."

During this time, the Earl fortified the town, probably building earthen ramparts. Dr. Kendrick, one of our distinguished citizens of the 19th century, found in 1850-51, some warrants of these days hidden in the thatch of an old half-timbered house at Houghton Green, and they throw light on some of the local happenings of this time. In one it requires the attendance of six carts and ten men to repair the works at Warrington after the siege.

We can well believe that the Parliamentarians would not leave the possession of so important a point as the Mersey crossing in Royalist hands without making some effort to capture it. In the spring of 1643, Sir William Brereton, a Cheshire man who had declared for Parliament, set out from Northwich to attack the Earl of Derby at Warrington. It was on Easter Monday that the advance guard of the Parliament forces approached the town from the south, "the Earl's men, only perceiving a small  body of troops, sallied out and met them on Stockton Heath, where only the timely arrival of Sir William with the main body of troops prevented a Parliamentarian defeat. The Royalists withdrew behind the town's ramparts, taking with them prisoners and colours, while their enemies remustered on the Heath.

Later in the same day, the Earl of Derby, using the captured colours as a camouflage, arranged for his men to advance in two parties. One was to go via the Causeway, and the other over Ackers Common, via the ford, thus creating a pincer movement on the army encamped on the Heath. These surprise tactics proved successful, and Sir William's forces were routed. Tradition has it that many of the Puritan army who died on the Heath that day were buried in the graveyard at Hill Cliff, whilst others, according to the registers of Budworth Church, were buried there.

Sir William, however, attacked again within a few days. This time he sent part of his forces across the river at Hale, and, joined by reinforcements from Wigan, attacked Warrington from Sankey Bridge, and practically succeeded in taking the town, but the Earl of Derby set fire to it rather than let it fall into the hands of the enemy, threatening to destroy it completely, upon which Sir William withdrew his forces after besieging it for three days.

The Earl then left the defence of the town to a Colonel Norris. He, knowing the strategic value of the town, and realising that the Parliamentarians would make further efforts to secure it, set about its defence. Proof of this we have in two warrants found by Dr. Kendrick at Houghton Green, one of which we give in full. It was evidently sent out by courier to the Winwick constable with orders to pass it on.

"Whereas lately I directed my warrants to severall parts more adjacent for the calling in of all able men unto our ayd, but finding the Enemy was retraited, was very willing that the said men should return to their own houses. But nowe soe it is that this day I have received intelligence by 3 severall messengers that the enemy intends very speedily to assault us. This therefore in his Maj'ty's name straitley to charge and Comand you that forthwith upon receit here of you give notice and warning to all the able men w'thin yor Constableries that are within the age of 60 years and above the age of 16 years that they come unto this town of Warrington with their best armes and p'vision of meate for 4 dayes by 9 of the clock being 15th day of May.

E. NORRIS."

Endorsed on the back by the various constables as follows,
Seene and P'sured by Constable of Winwick and Hulme.
"   "   "   by Constable of Newton
"   "   "   "   "   of Haidoke and
speedilye sent away to Constable of Golborne, etc."

Here then was another duty of the constable. How many men they were able to supply is not stated, but Colonel Norris' informants were correct, for Sir William Brereton returned to Nantwich and from there despatched a force under Sir George Booth of Dunham Massey and Colonel Assheton of Middleton, to attack the town. This time they brought cannon with them, and in the words of an eye witness "played upon the town all that week." By the end of the week food was running short - evidently Norris' writs had not produced much result in the surrounding country - and on the Saturday, the different factors held a parley, when it was agreed that the town should surrender upon the condition that the captains and men should depart, but leave behind their arms, ammunition and provisions.

The town was now garrisoned for Parliament. After these stirring events there followed a period of comparative quiet, from fighting at any rate. But as men could not fight and look after their lands, and as a stage of siege could not be in progress without the land being neglected, the inhabitants

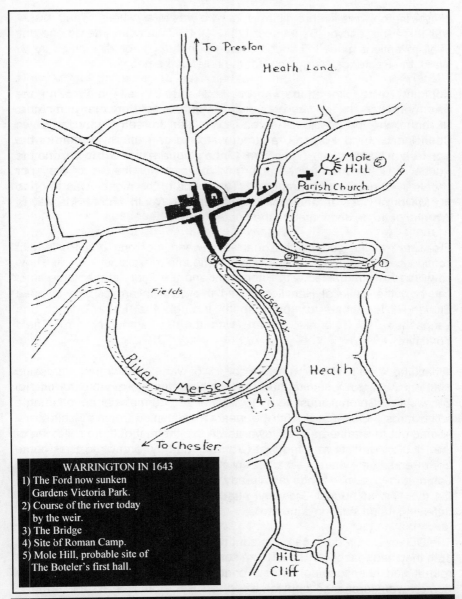

To Preston

Heath Land

Mole Hill ⑤

✝ Parish Church

Fields

Causeway

River Mersey

Heath

④

To Chester

Hill Cliff

WARRINGTON IN 1643
1) The Ford now sunken Gardens Victoria Park.
2) Course of the river today by the weir.
3) The Bridge
4) Site of Roman Camp.
5) Mole Hill, probable site of The Boteler's first hall.

Map of Warrington in 1643

of Warrington were in sore distress, famine was everywhere. Their misery was appalling, and on September l2th, 1644, Parliament ordered one half of all collections made in London churches that day to be distributed by Mr Ward, the Rector of Warrington, for the relief of the people.

Not only famine followed the war, but the Plague as well. In 1645, no one was permitted to go in or out of Manchester for many months. Nevertheless, the pestilence spread, and later the same year the Town Council of Liverpool ordered a street watch to be kept on account of the sickness at Warrington. Again in 1647 the plague visited the town, and the House of Commons ordered a further collection for the aid of the poor people in Chester and Warrington. Two-thirds of the money was to go to the Mayor of Chester, and the remainder to Mr Woolly and Mr Massey of Warrington to be distributed to the needy.

Elsewhere in the country the quarrel between the King and Parliament continued, until in 1648 the war again came into this district. We all know how Charles I bargained with Parliament and the Scots at the same time, and how the Duke of Hamilton raised the Scottish armies and invaded England. He chose to come south through the Lake District and Lancashire, as Colonel Lambert, with the Parliamentary army, held Yorkshire.

Reaching Kendal, Hamilton held a council of war. Some were for crossing the Pennines into Yorkshire, but Hamilton himself preferred to carry on into Lancashire. So on August 13th his army of 20,000 men began to struggle southwards. On August 16th he was at Preston, with part of his army spread out some fifteen miles towards Wigan, the rest of them still north of the Ribble. He little realised that Cromwell had by forced marches come from Pembroke, where he had been attacking the castle, and had joined Lambert in Yorkshire, and was already crossing the Pennines via Skipton. On the 17th of August Cromwell attacked the Scottish army at Preston, defeating it and splitting it into two.

The Duke was forced to carry on southwards with Oliver in pursuit. On the 18th they had reached Wigan. Here some were for making a stand, but the retreat had been carried on in a continuous downpour of rain, and the Scotch were drenched and famished, so Hamilton ordered the army to carry on to Warrington, where he hoped to hold the bridge and put the

Mersey between himself and Cromwell.

On the morning of Saturday the 19th, they had reached Winwick, and here, at Red Bank, the Scottish Foot made their last stand. They fought for several hours, but with 1,000 killed and 2,000 prisoners taken from them they were beaten. Hamilton fled through the town and over the bridge, leaving General Baillie and his foot regiment in the town to cover his flight. Cromwell set up his headquarters in the General Wolfe in Church Street, from where he sent the following report of his doings to Parliament.

"We prosecuted them home to Warrington Town, where they possessed the bridge, which had a strong barricade and work upon it, formerly made very defensive. As soon as we came thither I received a message from General Baillie desiring some capitulation, to which I yielded, considering the strength of the pass, and that I could not go over the Mersey within ten miles of Warrington. I gave him these terms. That he should surrender himself, all his officers, and soldiers prisoners of war, with all his arms and ammunition to me. I giving quarter for life and civil usage."

Winwick Church where many soldiers sought refuge

Warrington parish register cryptically records the battle as follows:--

> *"Memorandum Ye Lieftenant General Crumwil!s forces*
> *did routt Duke Hamilton's army, and Sir Marmaduke*
> *Langdales force upon 16, 17, 18, 19 of*
> *August in the yeare 1648."*

Thus did Charles' last hope die here at Warrington, and our town had seen the beginning and the end of the struggle. But the aftermath of the struggle remained for some years after King Charles' execution. Trade was at a stand-still, and part of the town was a burnt out ruin as a result of the siege. We have already given some account of the conditions prevailing as a result of the war. Further horrors came in 1654.

Then the County Court of Chester was held in Northwich on account of the Plague in the town and at Warrington. In the museum is to be seen the Plague stone taken from the corner of the wall of the half-timbered house in Wash Lane. Money for people afflicted with the Plague in the house was placed in a mixture of vinegar and water in the stone's hollow centre in order to disinfect the giver.

The town settled down to life under the Republic. The countryside was weary of the struggle, but though the king was dead, his son was very much alive, and in spite of Cromwell"s campaign in Scotland and the defeat of the Scots at Dunbar, Prince Charles managed to collect an army, with which he invaded England in 1651. He followed the route of the Duke of Hamilton, but knowing this time that Cromwell had been left behind in Scotland. He had hopes that Lancashire would rise up for him, but all he saw were scowling faces and Lord Derby with a few troops who came to him from the Isle of Man.

All he had in front of him were some Lancashire and Cheshire levies under Major General Harrison, who wrote as follows from Bolton:

> *"August 15. This day about noon we received under-*
> *standing of their advance for Preston, and soon of the'.r*
> *design to get before us to the pass at Warrington, where*
> *we have about 3,000 foot waiting."*

The next day Harrison was encamped at Warrington, where he wrote:

"We are improving the time we have got before them here to spoiling of the fords and passes on the river, especially between us and Manchester, leaving those only open to them where, if they attempt a passage, we may be able to make opposition."

His opposition could not have been much, for Charles forced the passage of the bridge, nearly three years to the day that it had been the defeat of the Duke of Hamilton; and flushed with the victory, went on to his ultimate defeat by Cromwell at Worcester.

From then till the Restoration in 1660, the town had a garrison of troops quartered on it to help to secure the peace of the countryside. In that year the constables of Warrington made the following return of arms in their hands to the Deputy Lieutenants of Lancashire.

Muskets and Pistol barrells without stocks	*39*
Muskets with stocks	*8*
Old swords	*12*
Iron caps	*21*
Suits of Armour	*9*
Drums	*1*
Muskets ready fixed	*3*
Swords that are dressed	*4*

So ended the war in this district, and after seeing the tide of battle ebb and flow around the town, let us now turn to its domestic affairs during the century.

A map in Dr. Kendrick's account of the siege of the town shows us the district in 1643. On it is shown the position of the ford across the river, at practically the end of Wash Lane, which in those days was one of the main routes from the south into the town. The course of the river was then very much different from what it is now. From the weir the river bent in a loop towards Latchford across Victoria Park, forming a peninsula along which the road went to the ford at the end of the loop. The narrow neck of this peninsula was only ten yards wide at high tide, and would constantly be eaten into by the force of the current. A very strong flood coming down in 1736 cut straight across the neck of the land, and the river became at this point as we know it to-day. In Victoria Park is a sunken garden, which I remember as a willow bed before it was made into a garden. A coppery coloured stream ran through it. The Park Keeper informed me one day that it was part of the old river bed.

From the bridge onwards the river followed its old course, the straight cut along Chester Road did not exist. Prior to 1624 the road south from the bridge followed the Knutsford Road to Wash Lane, then turned south across Ackers Common to Stockton Heath. All land in the immediate vicinity of the river, especially on its south side, was very low lying and subject to floods. Wash Lane and the Knutsford Road were raised up above the level of the fields.

In 1624, the bridge being in need of repair, it was found that the Earl of Derby had up to then repaired the bridge, and that he should do so again, but that such repairs would not be much use unless there was a safe and secure approach from the south.

Lord Delamere, first earl of Warrington

Two local men, Sir Thomas Ireland and Mr Marbury, then said that they would give the necessary land for the construction of a causeway, raised on arches, from Wilderspool to the bridge, the road to Chester then turning off along Greenall's Avenue. The Causeway is shown on the map, and must have been built soon after 1624, and no doubt facilitated the movement of the troops and armies about the district in the succeeding years.

A glance at the map will show these, and also the size of the town. Houses are marked on each side of Bridge Street, Horsemarket Street, up to Bewsey Road, along Church Street, and part way along Sankey Street. For the rest it was open fields with a large heath to the north of the town, on which was a windmill. The town itself, though so near the river, would not be liable to flooding as the fields on the south, because the underlying sandstone came very near to the surface, raising the centre of the town to some fifty feet above the river level.

In 1673 Bonne the Topographer visited the town and describes it as follows:

> *"Warrington is situated on the River Mersey, over which*
> *is a curious stone bridge. It is a very fine and large town,*
> *which has a considerable market on Wednesdays for linen*
> *cloth, being much resorted to by Welshmen, and is of note*
> *for its Lampreys."*

It is difficult for us to realise that the river was in those days quite a considerable source of wealth to the town. Warrington fisheries, up to as

Wilderspool Causeway at the turn of the century

late as 1850, were of no mean importance. In that year the salmon fishery at the island by the weir was rented for £150. These fisheries go back a long time. At Thelwall in 1367 many men were brought before the court for obstructing the flow of the river with fish weirs. Then it would appear that there were fish yards at Penketh, Latchford, Walton, Sankey and Warrington.

These fish yards or weirs in the river would be a source of danger to navigation and many attempts were made to get rid of them, but they lasted till well into the nineteenth century.

Towards the close of the seventeenth century we find a new aspect of the town emerging. Its proximity to the rising port of Liverpool, and the expansion of the country's overseas trade was bringing more trade into the town, and not a few industries were beginning to be centred here. In 1662 a Bill was before Parliament to improve the River Mersey, but the growing port of Liverpool was jealous of its privileged position and opposed the Bill. Nevertheless headway was made later by private enterprise. In 1690 Mr Thomas Patten, of Warrington, had the river made navigable from Runcorn to Bank Quay. He had occasion to complain of the fisheries in this manner.

"You may well know the mischief that is done in the River Mersey, or at least have frequently heard what vast numbers of salmon trout are taken, so as to supply all the country and market towns twenty miles around, until the country is cloyed, and when they cannot get sale of them they give them to their swine."

It is important to understand that the rivers then formed practically the only way of carrying goods in bulk into the country. Roads were extremely bad, and the only goods traffic over them was by cart and by pack horse. We find Mr Patten arranging to have tobacco sent from Liverpool by boat up the river, then by cart to Stockport, where they would be split up into smaller parcels for carriage by pack horse into Yorkshire.

By the close of this century the town was beginning to emerge from the mediaeval country market town and to develop an industrial leaning, as it had done when it had flourished under the Romans. This industrialism was fostered and increased because of the town's geographical position on the river and on the borders of a vast region destined by its natural resources in coal and iron, and its great port looking westwards to the raw materials of the new world to become one of the great industrial regions of the kingdom. Of this growth to the present industrial town the succeeding chapters will be devoted.

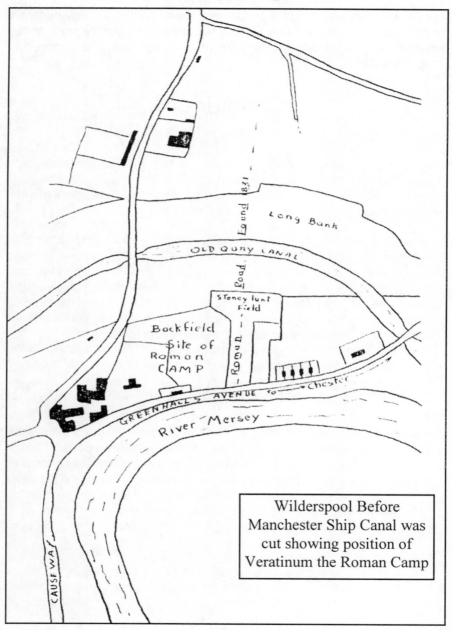

Wilderspool Before
Manchester Ship Canal was
cut showing position of
Veratinum the Roman Camp

Chapter VI
Warrington in the Eighteenth Century

By the time the eighteenth century had dawned, the social distress and ruination of the commerce of the town and country as a result of the civil war had been overcome, and a new era of commercial and industrial expansion was opened to its inhabitants.

Warrington's peculiar geographical position has been the prime factor in its development. The only easy and uninterrupted route into the growing industrial area of the county was through the town and over its bridge, and in this century the growing importance of this easy access swayed the town's industrial, social and historic life during this period, and its complex development causes us to divide the study of it into compartments for greater ease in reading, yet each is in some measure dependent upon the other. Up to now, purely historic data has been our main concern, so we will commence with that, passing on later to the newer aspects of the town.

Historical and Social

Even with a settled Government, war had not entirely deserted the district. The town long remained a garrison town for Government troops. Though the men were quartered on the inhabitants, they must have been pleased that Major Willis and his men were with them when in 1715 came the news that the Scots had once more crossed the border. They were defeated at Preston, and the people of Warrington must have witnessed the passing through of the rebel leaders on their way to Chester or London.

However, thirty years later the Pretender came south with an army, and this time there was more cause for alarm. It was essential that the bridge should be held, and he hurried on from Preston with that purpose. He was too late, for a regiment of Liverpool Blues arrived first and began to demolish the bridge with allspeed. A reconnaisance party of Highlanders, nearly 200 strong, approached the town and were taken prisoners. The main army was therefore forced, by the destruction of the bridge, to go through Manchester.

Some weeks later, the fleeing remnants of the army were seen passing through the district pursued by the Duke of Cumberland and the redcoats.

In the first year of the century, Warrington was described as a town famous for its trade and market, by a traveller and where malting was brought to as great a perfection as at Derby.

Old Warrington Market grew to be a thriving enterprise

A map dated 1772 shows that the town had not grown a great deal since 1643, though its commercial importance had increased. This is explained by the fact that most of the industries in the town were domestic industries carried on by the people in their own homes, and that the building of large works employing many hundreds of people, with consequent increase in housing, had yet to come. A careful study of the map reveals that there were houses in Church Street and Fennel Street, but that Battersby Lane, Lythgoes Lane and from there to the centre of the town was open fields.

Mersey Street had houses only on the left hand side, and the rest of Howley was fields up to the river. Between Mersey Street and Church Street was the quadrangle of the Academy. Bridge Street, being the principal thoroughfare, was lined on both sides with houses, having long gardens at their rear. St. Austin's, Bold Street, Rylands Street and Queens Gardens (except for Stanley Street) did not exist.

Horsemarket Street was built up on both sides, but Winwick Road had houses only on the left, the right hand side being fields right up to Pin Makers Brow. Sankey Street had houses up to the Park, whilst further along the river, where Crosfields now stands, were John Lyon's Quay and Colonel Patten's Quay, with Copper works and Glass works near by. These two, with a tanyard shown where the Odeon now stands, are the only works buildings shown.

The Market was then vastly different to the one we know today. Then it was known as the Market Square, and was divided down the centre by a row of houses into two parts, one larger than the other. Other houses stood all round the square. In the south-east corner of the smaller part was a low building of sandstone with approaching steps, and having a squat tower raised in stone pillars at one end. This was the Court house and housed the town bell.

Many writers of these times mention the markets and fairs held here. The formal opening of the fair was quite a local occasion. A procession was headed by the town crier in a fine livery, with a staff, a silver arm badge and silver laced cocked hat.

Accompanying him would be the four Manor constables, the deputy and steward and the company would wend its way to the Court house, where the fair would be declared open. Sales of horses and cattle took place as well as the buying and selling of other goods. For the amusement of the town and country folk who had flocked to the fair were strolling players, showmen, dwarfs, giants and mermaids, all accompanied by a great noise.

The bridge had four arches with recesses for the safety of foot passengers, and a watch house in its centre, purporting to have a dungeon in its basement. The river's banks were bordered by green fields, and fishing boats lay on its surface.

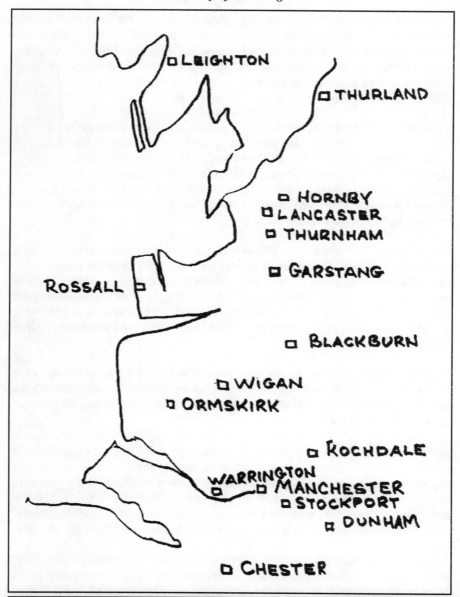

Tudor and Stuart Lancashire

We must not paint too rosy a picture, if we are to believe what Judge Curwen wrote about the town in 1777. "Its streets are narrow, dirty, and ill-paved, like many other towns, with a gutter running through the middle." On the other hand, The Universal Directory of Trade and Manufacture of 1792 describes the town as follows:--

"A large, neat, old built but populous and rich town,
with a considerable market on Wednesdays noted for
lampreys, and all sort of fish, corn, cattle, potatoes. The
entrance to Warrington is unpromising. The streets narrow,
long, ill-built, and crowded with carts and passengers, but
further on they are airy and of good width. A strong
mixture of mean buildings, handsome houses, as is the case
with most trading towns that experience a sudden rise. Its
markets are full of good country tradesmen. In the river
are caught sturgeons, green backs, millets, seals, sand eels,
lobsters, shrimps, prawns, and the best and largest cockles
in all England."

J. Aikin, writing of the History of Manchester and its surroundings in 1795, describes the town as "The usual effect of commercial opulence rising in a place of antiquity."

We must remember that the standard of our time is not the same as it was in the eighteenth century. People were used then to rougher treatment. Life was more callous, and punishment heavy for small crimes.

One writer declared that the road from Warrington to Chester was a gruesome sight with three gibbets on it.

While in 1790 the post-boy carrying the mails from Manchester was murdered near Woolston millpool, and the culprit, when found guilty at Lancaster Assizes, was sentenced to be hanged in chains near the scene of the crime.

Nevertheless, the streets with their black and white houses; the people in the dresses of those days, coats with full skirts having pockets with ornamented flaps on the outside, breeches with buckles on the knee, and large buckled shoes, wigs and three-cornered hats; the sedan chairs going from house to house; would have made a picturesque scene could we but have looked in on it.

An 18th century shopkeeper

The religious life played an important part in the town during this century. In the times of Cromwell a Puritan minister naturally held the living of the church. With the Restoration, however, came a reversion, and in 1662 the Act of Uniformity was passed. The minister, Robert Yates, was thrown out of the living for not conforming to the Prayer Book. He carried on his preaching, however, in his own and the houses of his congregation, though under great difficulty, for the Five Mile Act had banished those nonconforming ministers to five miles from their former churches. Later indulgence was granted them provided they obtained a licence. Yates was licensed in 1672, and also obtained permission to preach in his own house. A few months later he took out a licence for meetings to be held in the court house. With the accession of William of Orange to the English throne, more toleration was given and many chapels and meeting houses were erected.

The Warrington Nonconformists took over a barn belonging to a blacksmith and farmer at the back of Sankey Street. Here, in 1702, they built Cairo Street Chapel. These goodly folk and others in the country felt that the time was ripe for establishing a school or academy, as the founder said, "For the education of ministers free to follow the dictates of their own judgments in the enquiries after truth."

No doubt the Boteler Grammar School did not cater for their needs, being of the National Church.

So in 1757 the Rev. J. Seddon, the minister, started the school in the academy building at Bridge Foot, but in those days it had gardens extending along the river bank. Pupils grew in numbers, and five years later more commodious premises were taken in Academy Street. Here there was a quiet square surrounded on three sides by distinctive buildings and closed on the remaining side by iron railings having an arched gate, which is still preserved by the side of the present building.

Warrington Town Hall

Warrington Academy building

The first principal was Dr. Taylor he had Dr. Aikin and his son as assistants. Dr. Aikin lived in Dial Street in the house which bears a commemorative tablet. When J. Seddon died in 1770, Dr. Enfield came as Rector of the church and principal, and remained thirteen years until it was closed. With Dr. Enfield were associated three famous tutors. The first and foremost being Dr. Priestley, the discoverer of oxygen, who was tutor in natural sciences and Latin from 1762 to 1767. He was followed by Dr. Reinhold Forster, who left in 1772 to accompany Captain Cook, the explorer, as the naturalist on his second voyage round the world.

The other tutor was the Rev. Gilbert Wakefield, a great theological scholar. One can hardly say that they were overpaid for their work. They received a fee of £100 a year, and two guineas from each student who attended their lectures. Some of the pupils lived in the school, others as boarders with the tutors, paying them £15 a year, or £18 if they stayed on during the two months vacation. Towards the close of the school's period here the type of pupil fell off and a mischievous lot were enrolled. They were not amenable to discipline, being the sons of Jamaican planters, and Irishmen. They evidently believed in student's rags, for one morning all the landlords of the local inns awoke to find that all their signs had been changed round, while residents in Bank Street were disturbed at night by ghostly noises.

Things became so bad that in 1786 it was decided to close the Academy. It was later reopened in Manchester, then taken to York, after which it returned to Manchester, moved again to London, and finally became the Manchester College, Oxford. In spite of its later bad name in the town, the Academy had a considerable influence on the literature and scientific studies of the times, and played no small part in their advancement. Under its influence William Eyres, who had a printing house in Horsemarket Street, produced many books for the tutors and others. The most notable being John Howard's book on *The State of the Prisons of England.*

Eyres also published the first weekly paper produced in the town, *Eyres' Weekly Journal or Warrington Advertiser.* Promising days they must have seemed to many serious-minded people of the town, who had visions probably of seeing it develop as a seat of learning. But along with them were others whose vision was different, who saw here a natural site for a town of many industries, and by whose labours it so became.

Oliver Cromwell statue outside
Warrington Academy building

Industrial

The eighteenth century saw in England the beginning of its industrial status. Recent discoveries had led its people to begin the development of its abundance of raw material, while geographical exploration opened up to these growing industries the storehouse of natural products, mineral and vegetable, which the new countries contained. At the same time these industries demanded ever quicker transport, so that alongside this industrial growth was developed a countryside through which it was far easier to travel, and to travel in greater comfort, and with more speed, as well as to carry more in bulk per journey than had ever been possible in the preceding centuries. Warrington, as we shall see, was in the front of these changes.

The commercial centres of the country were, during this century, gradually moved from the south and east, where the ancient woollen manufactures had been centred, to the north and west. The new industries demanded power, which was here in abundance, first as water power in the many streams descending from the Pennine slopes, and later in the coal found in the Lancashire and Yorkshire plains.

The new colonies developing across the Atlantic were turning the eyes of commercially-minded folks from the east to the west, with a consequent shift in the shipping bases. The nearest port for Lancashire and the north was at Chester. It was from here that all national expeditions and individual travellers set out for Ireland. But increased shipping and the size of actual ships, and the silting up of the River Dee, as a result of its funnel shaped estuary causing the tide to pile up the sand and not scour it out as it ebbed, caused Chester to decline rapidly as a port. The trade was moved further down the estuary to Parkgate for a while, but this, too, became silted up.

The Dee, however, was not the only river, there was the Mersey. Its estuary is different from that of the Dee. A bottle neck causes the tide to force its way in and out of the wider part between Liverpool and Runcorn. While the incoming tide may bring in sand and silt, the rush outwards on the ebb of the enormous volume of water from its wide part keeps the entrance channel clean and deep, forming a natural harbour for large ships. Having such a naturally good harbour, facing the new countries in the west, and having as its hinterland the industrial north, it is no wonder then that Liverpool developed rapidly as a port. The character of our town was bound to be affected consequent upon its position and relation to these new areas of development.

We have already seen how one person describes it in 1700 "Famous for its trade and market." Twenty years later it is recorded that about £500 worth of linen is sold every market day. Thirty years later, in 1750, a Dr. Richard Pocock, journeying from Dublin, described the town as follows :-

> *"Warrington - a considerable town on the Mersey, chiefly supported by being a great thoroughfare, and by merchandise brought to it from Liverpool in flat-bottomed boats. Near the town is a smelting house for copper brought from Cornwall."*

In 1769 Daniel Defoe, touring Britain, visited the town and noted this aspect of it:

"In the town of Warrington and the villages around it, Sail cloth to the value of £70,000 per annum for the Navy, is made, in which and other coarse linens the wharehousemen of this town employ 10,000 persons. Here also are copper works, sugar works, glass houses and pin works."

The same year Arthur Young published his book on his *Six Months' Tour Through Northern England.* He noted that sailcloth employed 300 weavers, sacking 150, the pin works employed 2-3,000 children at from one shilling to two shillings a week, and another for shoes for export employed 4-500 men at nine shillings a week.

Then later, five years before the end of the century, J. Aikin wrote a *History of Manchester* and the surrounding country, in which he wrote of the town as follows:

"The usual effect of commercial opulence rising in a place of antiquity. Sail cloth made from hemp and flax. The raw material coming from Russia, via Liverpool, and then to Warrington by River."

Cotton, he found, was also introduced as an industry. Of the iron trade he found locks and hinges and files, and that an iron foundry had been set up. Vessels of 80 tons burden, he said, could come up to Bank Quay. The town was well equipped with coals from Haydock. Some 30-40,000 bushels of potatoes were shipped annually from Bank Quay. The population he gave as about 8,790.

Thus we see that a large variety of manufactures were carried on in the town, and it is proposed to examine some of these a little closer in order to complete the picture of life in the town at this time.

Probably that most frequently mentioned in contemporary records is the manufacture of linen, huckaback, sacking, sailcloth and fustians.

The manufacture of cloth, woollen and others, had been for many years one of the primary industries of the country, and one of its most important exports. In the early part of this century it was a domestic industry, the weaver working in his own home. With the introduction of machines, which did the work of five or six people, the industry became centred in various towns. The nearness of our town to the Irish flax, and to a ready market for sail cloth in the Liverpool ships, to some locally grown hemp, and cotton and hemp imported from America and Russia, led to a concentration of the industry here. Probably, as elsewhere, it first started in the homes of the people to supplement their earnings from other jobs.

James Croston, in his *History of Lancashire*, remarks that coarse linens and checks formed the first manufacture, giving way to a species of table linen called Huckaback, which was later succeeded by sailcloth making. As a home part-time occupation, a good weaver could make eight shillings at his loom. The weaver being dependent on the domestic spinner. It required six spinners to keep one weaver going. When the multiple looms were introduced they rang the death-knell of the home weaver, and caused them to give it up, or give up their other occupations and become full timers working in a mill. These mills were small at first when they were driven by water power, but later increased in size as the motive power of coal and steam began to be used.

Arthur Young, in his account of his visit to our town already given, goes on to give a little fuller account of the manufacture of cloth in the town as follows.

"At Warrington, the manufacture of sailcloth and sacking is very considerable. The first is spun by women and girls, who earn twopence a day. It is then bleached by men earning ten shillings a week. Next it is wound by women earning two shillings and sixpence a week, and warped by men who earn ten shillings and sixpence a week. Lastly it is weaved by men earning nine shillings, and women earning five shillings a week. Sailcloth employs 300 weavers, sacking half that number. There being twenty spinners and two or three other hands to every weaver."

Fustians, made from linen warp and cotton weft, and fustian cutting was also carried on, and in Lymm it is to be noticed that quite a few rows of houses have third stories now disused, with steps on the outside leading to them. This third storey was one long room running over the tops of all the houses in the row, and was used in the fustian industry. The workers probably living in the houses below.

94

Sugar refining was also mentioned. Throughout England in those days sugar was a luxury, until the increasing use of tea and coffee brought it into the list of principal foods. It is estimated that in 1700 the amount consumed in the whole country was only 10,000 tons.

Tanning, too, in its early establishment, was practically a one man industry. Its settlement here was no doubt due to the plentiful supply of skins from the farming regions of Lancashire and Cheshire, to a good water supply, plentiful supply of oak bark, and its nearness to the Cheshire salt mining district. The industry had long been established, for in 1633-5 the Warrington tanners were known to have corresponded with those of Lancaster, Wigan, Preston and Blackburn for better conditions.

Watchmaking was also of importance here. Living here, and carrying on their business for a while, were two famous watchmakers. John Harrison, the inventor of the compensating pendulum, won the Government's prize of £20,000 for the first successful chronometer to ascertain longitude correctly. John Kay, a watch maker, who was later associated with Richard Arkwright, the inventor of the flying shuttle, and Peter Lithelland, inventor of the lever watch, lived here.

The other most important industry of those days was the metal trade. The metal trade of the town and district had long been established, and the craftsmen were renowned for their skill. Three important branches of the industry were established here, file and tool making, copper, and pin making.

In the middle of this century the iron and steel workers were scattered about the country side, as the textile workers were. There was no definite centre until, like the textile industry, the introduction of machines, and the use of steam power, made possible the building of large works, thus bringing the scattered workers to some central point in some convenient town.

In a book, *An Eighteenth Century Industrialist,* T. Ashton has shown how this came about in the case of the file industry of Peter Stubs. Anyone wishing to study it further cannot do better than read this book. Here we shall only give a brief outline of the industry.

It appears that Peter Stubs' father was a dresser of tanned leather. By the time the son was twenty-one in 1777, it was evident that he was not going to enter the tanning trade like his father, for he was by then already established as a file maker, and later combined it with the keeping of the White Bear Inn in Bridge Street. A London watchmaker wrote in 1773 that Lancashire tools were the best executed. In the Cabinet Cyclopedia of 1833, Dr. Lardner says, *"The acknowledged superiority of Lancashire files has been already mentioned - to files may be added chisels, graving tools, watch and clock making tools, hand vices, pincers, metal and wire gauges, cutting pliers, etc. The metropolis of this trade is Warrington. In this line even Birmingham yields the palm of superiority to Warrington."*

By 1788 Stubs was employing filemakers not only in the town, but also in many of the surrounding villages of Lancashire and Cheshire. These people had small workshops attached to their homes. Mr. J. Westbrook, in his book on Stockton Heath, records that file cutters lived and worked in Toll Bar Row, while I personally know of one such small workshop attached to a house in Appleton in which the owner made pliers by hand up to a few years ago.

Warrington Bridge - the gateway to Lancashire

Jas. Nasmyth, inventor of the steam hammer, says in his autobiography, *"Mr Stubs proceeded to give me an account of the origin of the peculiar system of cottage industry in his neighbourhood. It appears that Hugh de Lupus, William the Conqueror's master of arms, settled in North Cheshire shortly after the conquest. He occupied Halton Castle, and his workmen resided in Warrington and the adjacent villlages of Appleton, Widnes, Prescot and Cuerdley. There they produced coats of steel and iron weapons under the direct superintendence of their chief. The manufacture thus founded continued for many centuries. When the use of armour was discontinued, these workmen turned to more peaceful purposes. The cottage workmen made the best of files and steel tools. Their talents became hereditary, and the manufacture of wire in all its forms is most peculiar to Warrington and its neighbourhood. Most of the workmen's peculiar names for tools were traceable to old Norman French words."*

To this type of worker Stubs supplied the raw material. Pewter on which the files were cut, metal bars, malt dust, oil, and salt. His public-house formed a convenient centre for distribution and collection, as well as providing the malt.

Each week or fortnight the finished files were brought in and the workers credited with their value, less 25 per cent. He specialised in making small files; when customers wanted large ones he obtained them from friends in Sheffield. The worker's family often worked with him. Some families did the complete job from start to finish, others sent cut files in to Stubs for hardening, yet others confined themselves to forging and others to cutting. Hammers and pliers were also made for him, and next to filemaking, awlmaking for the tannery trade was another output.

Later on he established his works in Scotland Road, in 1802, and proceeded, if possible, to get the outworkers to come and work for him there. To these he often had to advance travelling money, pay off debts they had contracted to other masters before they would release them, and also find them lodging. Military service sometimes took them away unless he was prepared to pay from £7 - £8 for a substitute. He also started to take on apprentices. One such, William Metcalfe, a lad of 12, was bound for seven years. His father agreeing to provide good wholesome food, clothes, and a doctor in case of sickness, while Stubs agreed to give him a week's holiday at Christmas, and one shilling at the time of the Warrington

Fair, and a wage of two shillings, rising to seven shillings a week in his last year. In those days the town's apprentices had holidays at Christmas, Good Friday, Easter, Ash Wednesday, and Shrove Tuesday.

Stubs obtained his raw material chiefly from Sheffield, Rotherham, Newcastle, and even Scotland. The manufactured article he disposed of through factors, chiefly in Ashton in Makerfield, but later he supplied his customers direct.

In those days, too, innkeepers made their own ales. Stubs used to sell malt and ales to others. He bought barley and hops to make his own ales. As in his file business, he bought from many sources. He rented two malt kilns in Sankey and employed agents to buy grain in Cheshire.

The second important metallurgical industry established here was that of copper smelting. It was introduced into Lancashire by the Patten family. They built their works at Bank Quay about 1717. In our second chapter we have seen how the Romans worked copper in Wales at Great Ormes Head, and at Alderley Edge, Cheshire. This latter mine was reopened in 1755 and later taken over by Mr Patten and worked with some profit. Round about 1790 a Mr Radcliffe reported that the mine was going well, but the lead was not in one place. The copper continues good. Eight women were employed in dressing the copper and a woman came from Derbyshire to wash the lead.

With the gradual falling off of this mine the Pattens went elsewhere for their ore, to Cornwall and Anglesey. Here in the north-east corner of Anglesey was found, in 1768, a whole hill of copper ore, known as Parys Mountain. It quickly became the largest mine in Europe, and at the end of the century was yielding some 3,000 tons of copper a year. The fact that the Pattens had improved the Mersey navigation in 1690, and again in this century, enabled them to ship the ore direct to Bank Quay.

Curious uses were made of the slag obtained from the smelting. It was used as the foundation of the road to Manchester when it was repaired. It was also cast into the shape of bricks and used by Col. Patten to build the foundations of his new house, now the Town Hall.

The vast derelict remains of the Parys Mountain copper mines can be seen to-day by any visitor to Amlwch, as well as the decaying houses round the old port where lived the miners at the smelting works also built there. All bear witness to the activities of the eighteenth century. We find a vivid account of these in A. Aikin's *Journal of a Tour in N. Wales*, written in 1797. He says:--

"We had no difficulty in distinguishing the mountain, for it is perfectly barren from the summit to the plains below - the nearer we approached the scene the more penetrating became the fumes of sulphur. Here are comparatively few shafts, the greater part being quarried out so as to leave a vast excavation open to the day. Every corner resounds with the noise of the pick axes, the edges lined with workmen drawing up the ore from below."

The chief sources of copper came from the ore broken by hammers at which job women and children were employed, and copper sulphate in solution pumped from the mine. This solution was run from the mine into pits, like tannery pits, which can still be seen to-day rising in tiers up the mountain side. Into the solution in these pits was placed scrap iron, the sulphate combining with the iron and depositing the copper.

Some of the crude copper was smelted at Amlwch and some sent to Liverpool, Warrington and Swansea. The rough copper then cost £2 10s. 0d. a cwt. The mines employed some 1-2,000 miners and 90 smelters, who earned from one shilling to one shilling and eightpence a day.

Amlwch, before the discovery of the mine, was a village of no more than half a dozen houses. In 1797 it had 4-5,000 people living in it, sloops and brigs of 100-150 tons carried the copper from its port. The Anglesey company also had a copper and brass works at Holywell. Here the copper, sent in the form of pigs from smelting works at Amlwch, Liverpool, Warrington and Swansea, was made into plates for the bottoms of wooden ships, into basins, copper wire, brass dishes and shallow pans. These latter were exported to China by the East India Company for drying tea on, and to Africa, where they were used for making salt from sea water by evaporation in the sun. The power for this works, which Aikin describes as vast, was obtained from a water wheel driven by the water issuing from St. Winifred's Holy Well. The same power was used to work corn mills, cotton works and forges.

In 1755, Chamberlayne wrote that Warrington is much noted for a large smelting house for copper, and also a large sugar house. Pocock, in his journey through the town, as we have already quoted, makes mention of the copper house, and goes on to say: *"It turns to good account here by reason of a great supply of coals. It is first burnt twelve hours then cast, afterwards burnt twelve more hours, then melted a third time and then cast into pigs. Some is sent to Holywell to be beaten into plates and some to Cheadle in Staffs, to make brass."*

Communications

As already stated, the improvements in industry led to better means of communications, which in turn helped still further to add to the town's industrial growth.

Up to now the only means of travelling about the country and conveying goods from place to place was by road, or by a navigable river if one was available. Let us see briefly what state the transport system about Warrington was in as this century opened. First, the river had been made navigable from Liverpool to Runcorn, then by Mr Patten from Runcorn to Bank Quay. But as the port of Liverpool had hardly emerged from the fishing village stage (the first dock was not made till 1715), the river traffic was small, as well as the boats that used it. The roads were in a deplorable condition, in many cases mere tracks. The pack horse was practically the only overland means of transporting goods. We have already seen in the last chapter how Mr Patten had to make use of them. The Manchester cotton manufacturers of those days had also to use this means to get their cotton from London.

In 1732, and for a long time afterwards, it was laid upon each individual parish to maintain the roads through it. Mr Hodgkinson, in his paper on *Highways about Grappenhall*, tells us that the parish had to appoint a surveyor to serve without pay for a year, that the inhabitants of the parish were obliged to work four, later six consecutive days each gear without pay on the roads. Material for construction was obtained locally, marl stones, blocks of sandstone, and later the copper slag. A little later in the century carriers' carts took the place of the pack trains, and coaches were provided for passengers, but on the badly rutted, slush-ridden surfaces the going was intolerably slow. After the 1745 rebellion, when General Wade showed what good road construction was by building the roads that subdued Scotland, improvements began to be made in the roads of England. The improvements, however, were done through the Turn Pike Acts, which were not popular, as it meant that the improver of that section of the road often had the right to levy tolls. Two Turn Pike Trusts were made locally - in 1752, from Mere to Warrington, and in 1767 from Chester to Wilderspool. That these improvements were beneficial we can gather from the statement made by Henry Homer in his *Enquiry into Public Roads,* written in 1767. *"There never was a more astonishing revolution accomplished. The carriage of grains, coals, merchandise, etc., is in general conducted with little more than half the number of horses it formerly was."*

In 1756 the first stage waggon was run from London to Kendal through the town. The following year a flying coach was run to London in three days. Passengers from Liverpool or Manchester wishing to join the coach had to come to Warrington. In 1767 a coach direct from Liverpool to Manchester was started.

An 18th century coach
on a lane in Cheshire

By 1774 stage coaches from Liverpool to London passed through twice daily on six days of the week. The greatest quantity of goods was, however, carried by carrier's cart.

As the century advanced the road transport was gradually improved, but locally the carriage of goods by road suffered a decline when the canals were constructed. First, the river was made navigable to Manchester in 1720 by making cuts across some of its bends. Howley Quay was built in 1761. The transport of goods by boat from the town to Liverpool depended upon the state of the tides, and boats were often held up waiting. To overcome this waiting for the tide the Old Quay canal was cut in 1801 from Manor Locks to Runcorn. On this the Mersey and Irwell Navigation Company ran not only flats carrying goods, but also swift packet boats for passengers only. They were drawn by two or three swift horses with red jacketed jockeys riding them.

They were timed to catch the ebb tide at Runcorn. The lockmaster held up all other traffic for them. At the same time that the Mersey was improved the River Weaver was made navigable to Runcorn, thus opening up the Cheshire salt fields to the industries of Lancashire.

The vagrances of river navigation, along with the fact that several other growing industrial districts like Birmingham and the Potteries were not near to such river improvement schemes, led to the building of canals. The first was the Sankey Canal, sanctioned in 1755, as the improvement to the Sankey Brook was being found impracticable. This was followed by the construction of the famous Bridgewater Canal, opened in 1761. Here too, both passenger and goods traffic was carried. Thus, with the construction of these two canals there was inaugurated an era of canal building, so that by the end of the century the country was better supplied with water transport than it had been with road transport at the beginning. Warrington, as we have seen, was a nodal point in the road system of northern England, and was by its geographical position so placed that when the traffic was deflected to the canals it benefited very greatly from these as well, since it now had communications with other industrial districts from Lancashire. To its unrivalled facilities for cheap transport then, must be attributed, during these and the succeeding years, its many and varied industries.

Chapter VII
The Nineteenth Century

The rise of many industries in the town during the 18th century continued during the succeeding century, and the town's industrial character was consolidated by this steady expansion and the introduction of still newer industries. This century saw great advances in the realm of industry and also the Industrial Revolution as it is termed by historians.

The awakening of the country to the wealth of resources and raw materials had already taken place, as we saw in the previous chapter. Its vast effect on our town manifested itself in changes in the industrial world. The use of steam power was introduced, new machines were invented to do the work of many people. New roads and canals opened up the country and brought a bigger demand for manufactured goods. A network of railways spread over the land, new markets overseas clamoured to be supplied with British goods, and the Napoleonic War, the Crimean and Boer wars increased the demand for manufactured goods and weapons of destruction. And Warrington, because of its geographical position and many industries, was carried along by the advancing flood of industrial activity.

The manufacture of goods at home was ousted during this period by the construction of works buildings. Only the richer manufacturer could lay out the necessary capital on new machinery, and having once installed it, could supply the market with so much material that household workers were unable to compete with this output and gradually drifted into the new mills.

This replacement was not a sudden change, but gradually took place throughout the period, increasing towards the end of the century as the Industrial Revolution gathered impetus, but this period was one of much distress, as the workers had no organisation and their working conditions were rigidly controlled by their masters.

Warrington's famous Golden Gates outside the town hall

Parr Hall, home of Warrington variety shows and exhibitions

We have already seen how some of the new industries were carried on, and here is another example of the life of a Warrington worker of those days.

Peter Stubs left his file and tool making business to his sons when he died. They increased their activities by starting a pin manufactury, not by any means the only one in the town at that time. In 1814, according to *The records of a pin manufactury,* written by T. Ashton, they entered into partnership with one of their father's riders or travellers, and set up premises rented at £10 a year. They purchased whitstones, drawing blocks, whitening pans, shears, etc., in quantity from the ironmongers. Adults and children were employed, there being abundant labour of the latter in the town, but often adult workers were transferred from other pin manufacturing centres, the chief of which was at Gloucester. From here, for example, they brought at their own expense, six women, who travelled to the town in the Bang-up Coach from Birmingham.

All classes of workers were paid piece rates, Stubs again supplying the material and crediting the worker with the finished product and waste.

The raw brass wire came from the Cheadle Brass Company set up about the time that the Pattens commenced their copper works at Bank Quay. The Cheadle Brass Foundry long used the water power from the River Churnet, and purchased their raw material, copper pigs from the Pattens or from the Anglesey companies direct.

The wire drawers were paid about 20/- a week, and often hired their wire drawing blocks from Stubs. The wire was then cut and pointed by others, and their average wage was 1/1 for lOlbs of pins.

The pins of those days had no solid heads. These were made from little coils of finer brass wire rivetted to the pin. This heading was done by children and women. They received about 2/- to 6/- per week, children getting 1/ - to 1/6 a week. These children were hired for 50 weeks, a period just less than twelve months, this being necessary to give outsiders the right to poor relief. Parents often borrowed money on the credit of their children's labours. These children often worked for a woman who ran a heading shop, obtaining her equipment from Stubs, Wood & Co. These workshops earned for their mistresses the sums of £1 to £1 10s. a week, so the unfortunate children working therein could not have earned much. After heading, the Pins were whitened by two or three men, earning £1 a week. The better grade pins were sold in neat rows on paper, another job done by children. In 1816 the firm paid an outworker threepence halfpenny a dozen for filling the paper sheets with pins.

Even though we may consider these conditions of work to be very bad, the workers did not, for there were no strikes as at other centres. The firm treated their workers well, even to Christmas boxes, and Shrove pennies for the children. In 1824, Edward Baines wrote his *Directory of Lancashire*, and in it devoted a considerable section to our town in that year, and from which we can construct the following picture of its life and activities.

Then it consisted of five parishes, Burtonwood, Fearnhead, Rixton, Woolston and Warrington. The whole having a population of some 16,698. Of this total Warrington had some 13,000 people, and 2,832 houses. This shows nearly double the number of people given by J. Aikin for 1795.

Offsetting the conditions under which large numbers of children were employed in the manufactures during the week-day, Baines tells us that in 1825 2,520 of them attended at the Sunday schools attached to the various churches. In fact, the town was in the forefront of the Sunday school movement founded by Robert Raikes. St. James' had opened their school in 1779. These, with a Blue Coat School, and a female Charity School, provided the only education in the town for the poorer classes.

Its fairs and markets were still held. We have mention now of a Town Hall in Irlam Street, the old Market Hall, two Cloth Halls, one adjoining the Market Hall and one in Buttermsrket Street. On the ground floor of these buildings, fustians, hardware, linen, drapery and other goods were sold, especially on market days. Gas light was provided for the town by a company set up in 1821.

The town was still governed by four constables. These, with other local officers, were still elected every October by the Manor Court, the Lord of the Manor then being Mr John Blackburne, M.P., who had purchased the Manor from the descendants of the Booth family. The tolls of the markets still went to the Lord of the Manor, who had, however, let them out on lease to a Mr Pickmere.

On the industrial side changes had taken place. The coarse linens had given way to huckaback or table linen, which was in turn giving way to sail cloth making. The sails of Nelsons fleet came in large quantities from here. But owing to the cessation of the war its place was rapidly being taken by the manufacture of cotton yam, calico, velveteen and fustians.

Sugar refining had gone, as had also the copper works, probably both put out of action by a gradual monopoly established by combines in more favourable places like Bristol and South Wales.

The various branches of the iron trade, the glass works, the tanneries and breweries were all still flourishing, whilst another innovation found in 1825 is that in that year seventeen steam engines were at work. Six of them creating power for spinning cotton, two for power weaving, three in the glass works, one in wire drawing, one in a tannery, and the last four in driving corn mills.

The town was at this time a great centre for the manufacture of various types of glass ware. It is not known who was the

Blackpool

Wigan Town

Southport

Raw Materials In
Manufactured
Goods Out

Birkenhead

Liverpool

Widnes

Manchester

Runcorn

Warrington

Chester

Goods
from
The Black Country
and
Potteries

To London

Coal and Iron

Salt

Cotton Manufacture

Warrington and its
Industrial Relations

107

first glass master. Both court and crown glass ware were made, and quite a few specimens of this work are in the museum. Baines, in his Directory, gives a full list of the inhabitants engaged in various industries in 1824. Here we shall only state a few of them to give a pointer to the numerous activities carried on. There were five basket makers using willows and osiers grown in the low-lying parts surrounding the town. Seven blacksmiths catered for the large use of horses. Six braziers were also to be found in the town. Seven calico manufacturers, five chairmakers, five coopers, seven firms engaged in cotton spinning, seven corn millers, seven curriers or dressers of tanned leather. Three people were engaged in dyeing cotton or other cloths.

In School Lane, J. Povey made files, while Stubs' firm did likewise in Scotland Road, and K. Wait in Winwick Street, and S. Waite in Pinners Brow. In Orford Lane J. Charnock dressed flax. Fustians, an important branch of the cloth trade, was carried on by ten firms, while twelve firms were concerned with the various sides, manufacturing and cutting, etc., of glass ware. There were two soap boilers, three tallow chandlers, three iron and brass founders, two nail makers, and three firms engaged in making pins, four rope makers, seven sail cloth makers, and three wire workers. Of all the list of names given by Baines, only a few are found in business today.

All these manufacturers were helped in disposing of their goods by excellent communications by land and water to many other parts of the country.

"Between sixty and seventy coaches, on an average, pass through Warrington every day. And the principal streets are kept by them in a continued state of animation."

The principal coaches leaving the town for Liverpool, Manchester, London, Birmingham and Chester, appear to have started from one of the following inns - The George, Bridge Street, The Nag's Head, The Talbot and The White Hart, all in Sankey Street, as well as The Lion in Bridge Street. Very busy scenes must have been witnessed in these inn yards as the coaches came clattering in, or sallied forth to the sounding toots of the coach guard's horn.

The Lion Inn on Bridge Street from where coaches left the town

Seven large carrying firms had agents in the town, carrying goods to all parts of the country. While from one or other of the town's eighty-four inns some twenty-three carriers' wagons set out, mostly on Mondays, Wednesdays, Fridays or Saturdays for the many neighbouring towns and villages.

The canals and the river, too, were busy with goods and passenger traffic. The Old Quay Company still worked boats up and down the river to Manchester and Liverpool, as well as along their canal from Manor Locks to Runcorn. This canal was seven and a half miles long and avoided the tidal section of the river. There was keen rivalry between this company and the Duke of Bridgewater's company. The former even lowered their charges by half in an effort to crush the traffic on the Duke's canal. Both companies ran Packet boats for passengers.

On the river, the Old Quay Company's packet arrived daily at twelve noon at Warrington Bridge from Manchester. To us it would seem an unusual sight to see passengers disembarking from a boat at the Bridge, but then it was an every day occurrence. Another boat on their canal landed passengers at Black Bear Bridge, or took them on for the journey to Runcorn. The notice says that on its return at one o'clock passengers are embarked for Manchester. Passengers on these packets for Stockton Heath were landed at the Saracen's Head, Wilderspool.

On the Duke's canal at Stockton Heath, the Manchester and Runcorn packets met at the Coach and Horses Packet House every day at one o'clock. Besides these regular services both companies ran extra boats to Runcorn to meet the steam packet boats from Liverpool according to the state of the tides.

As the century advanced, so did the industrial wealth of the country expand. New inventions and processes increased the demands for all types of manufactured goods. Trade naturally fluctuated from time to time, but throughout there was a steady increase. Our town shared in all these aspects of commercial life.

The tanneries expanded from single operatives into works covering large areas. Many new ones were set up, including John James, tanner, of Mersey Street; Vernon Street Tannery and Waring's Tannery. This latter firm was started in 1836 by Arthur Waring, as a tanner's offal, sizing, and hair merchant. Coming from London, he acquired a site in Winwick Road called Haydocks Yard. He rented fields near to the Barracks, where hair for plastering purposes was spread out to dry. The tanning industry was, by the end of the century, one of the principal activities of the town, and had gradually extended its demands for raw material to well beyond the immediate counties to the vast cattle regions forming in the new countries beyond the seas.

In the iron industry, new railways, steel ships, and the greater use of machines in all types of factories created a big demand, and called forth new iron works to make them. Messrs. Tayleur, engineers, of Warrington, built one of the early iron ships at their Bank Quay foundry. The John Tayleur, launched in 1853, a fine iron clipper, 225 feet long, was towed by tugs to Liverpool, and handed over to her owners, who intended her for the Australian passenger trade. In January, 1854, she left Liverpool on her first and last voyage, carrying 660 people.

The *Warrington Gazette* gave the following account of her last moments.

"She made fair weather till she got off Holyhead, when the wind headed her and a squall came on with dense fog. On Saturday morning the man at the wheel called he thought he saw land looming. The ship's course was altered, and while on this course about half-an-hour afterwards, the man on the look-out cried 'Breakers on the starboard bow.' It was then blowing heavily. The sheets of the head sails were let go, but in about twenty minutes she struck with great violence on a reef of rocks running out from a creek to the east of Lambey Island."

-*Guardian,* Oct. 28, 1854.

It was the latter half of this century that saw the rise of "The Wire." Perhaps one of the oldest wire workers of the town was Mr Greening. The family had been needle makers and wire drawers at Tintern Abbey during the seventeenth century. The founder of the existing firm came from Tintern in 1779 and established his works here. In 1807 Greenings took into partnership a Mr Rylands and carried on business at the Bridge Foundry. They invented the first machine for wire weaving by steam power. The partnership was dissolved in 1843, Mr Nathaniel Greening setting up separate business.

Another early wire worker was Mr Houghton, who set up a works about 1780 which continues in operation today, since 1926, however, as part of the combine British Wire Ropes.

The great firm of Rylands came into being in 1805. It was originally started to manufacture sailcloth, but later switched over to wire making.

White Cross Wire was built in 1864 on its present site by the side of the main L.M.S. Railway. The products of all these firms, in the form of wire, wire netting, wire nails, barbed wire, springs, netting, ropes, etc., have been sent all ever the world; have played their part in all the new advances in the steel and iron trade; in fencing large areas of the earth's surface; the nailing of boxes containing the world's produce; in the defence of great armies and shipping, and most recently in the defensive fencing of our own island.

These later years saw, too, the establishment of firms engaged in the making of heavy iron goods, steel plates for ship building, girders for

111

...and a ... ... which is vital ... ... was
... ... to ... ... the ... of the be ... The
... materials of the ... ... both an ... and vegetable
were either found near ... or could easily be brought into the district so
that Warrington and its neighbours — Runcorn and Widnes - were able to
offer excellent sites for the establishment of chemical industries.

On May 11, 1814, George Crosfield, of Lancaster, wrote:
*"I left Lancaster on my way to Warrington, rested a night at Yarrow Bridge,
reached Warrington at twelve o'clock. The object of my journey was to
view some premises near Bank Quay suitable for a soapery, which
business our son Joseph seems to have a strong inclination for."* The
following year saw the establishment of that great firm.

In those early years every pan of soap was made in bond, the pans having
iron lids, which were fastened down and locked by excise officers every
night, until the duty on soap was removed in 1853. The raw materials used
included salt from Cheshire, caustic soda, animal fats, palm oil, soya bean
oil, whale oil, resin from the pines of India, America and France, and
perfumes, like otto of roses, from Bulgaria. The works steadily grew from
employing only 250 hands to well over 3,000, from producing 10,000 tons
a year to 120,000 tons, from goods brought by coach and boat to raw
materials brought by rail, ocean liners and motor vans; from selling in a
local market to selling in practically every grocer's shop in the world.

Warrington ales have long been famous, and we have seen how Stubs and
many of the other innkeepers brewed their own. But just as the
independent workers in tools, clothing and tanning were ousted by the

larger works, so the brewing of ales became an industry, and large breweries, like Walkers and Greenalls, came to be established.

The production of so many goods necessitated much packing before despatching.   And in those days packing meant wood.   Naylors established their saw mill in 1872 at Howley, buying local and imported timber. They saw immediately the value to their import trade of the Ship Canal when it was built, and so moved to their present site, thus allowing ships to come right up to their mills instead of having to break cargoes at Liverpool.

The old corn mills of the Lord of the Manor have now been replaced by modern buildings built by Faircloughs before 1830, and they now draw to their mills not only the grain of the county and the rest of England, but also that of Canada, U.S.A., Australia and the Argentine.

All these activities are fostered and pushed forward by further strides in means of communication, just as they had been in the early years by the coaches and the canals.   The carrying trade of the latter, and the passenger traffic of the former are now challenged by the new railways. Warrington, at the crossing of the lines running north from London, with those connecting Liverpool and Manchester, with Wales and the rest of Lancashire, was bound to benefit by being put so easily and readily into contact with the capital and other great industrial regions.

The competition between the railways, roads and canals was furious while it lasted.   But the speed of the new was bound to end in the death of the old ways.

The Old Quay Company sold their canal to the Mersey and Irwell Navigation for £10,000 in 1779.   They in turn, because of the speedier traffic on the Bridgewater Canal, had to sell out to that company in 1843 for £400,000.   Now the faster railways were taking all the Bridgewater Company's trade, and they were glad to sell the Bridgewater Trust to a syndicate of railway directors in 1872 for £1,250,000.

As the Industrial Revolution gathered impetus, so a great social change came over the country, and our town in particular. Large masses of people sprang up, as it were, overnight, and long established sites like Warrington increased in size enormously.

Up to 1840 most of the buildings in the town were found along the four main roads. But from then till the end of the century row after row, street after street of workers' houses were put up behind these main roads on the fields of Howley, Whitecross and Bewsey.

Baines put the population in 1824 at 13,000, but by the time the census was taken in 1861 it had risen to 26,431, and has increased steadily ever since, as this table shows:

1861	26,431
1871	32,144
1881	41,452
1891	55,288
1901	64,242
1911	72,178
1921	78,600
1931	79,317

Large numbers of people came from the country to the towns. Yet they had very little say in their own government, and in the wages and conditions of their labour. Up to 1832 the people of Warrington were not represented in Parliament, while Newton-le-Willows, by right of its ancient barony, sent two members to Westminster. With the new Reform Bill, however, some measure of representation was secured, but not for the masses. The vote went to the £10 householder. For this election it was proposed to make a Parliamentary borough out of Warrington, Latchford, and part of Thelwall. This borough is given in the report as having a population of some 18,184 living in 3,798 houses, only 973 of which were of the value of £10 a year or more. So out of that large number of people only 973 were entitled to a vote. The election took place on December 13, 1832, only 379 votes being polled altogether. The town's first M.P. being elected by a majority of 27.

Mr Hornby	203
Mr Blackburne	176

Not till later in the century, and after great agitation and more Reform Bills, did the general mass of the people get the vote.

So it was, too, in local government. The Lord of the Manor still nominated the town's officials, the constables, the market officials, etc., and only in 1847, when Warrington secured its incorporation, did its inhabitants obtain a voice in their own local government. Then was held the first municipal elections. Mr Beamont, that lover and historian of the town, became its first Mayor. With what pride he must have taken office, and with other citizens, have walked the bounds on September 10th of that year.

Social progress was gradually taking place, but as yet there were many blots. The leisurely life of the eighteenth century, and the independence of its craftsmen disappeared in the maelstrom of this industrial get-rich-quickly age. Life for the workers in the new towns was hard and bitter. The worker, his independence gone, was at the whim of his master if he had work, if not, he had to sit idle while his wife and children worked long hours to support them. Combination Acts were passed preventing them from combining to ask for a rise in wages. Magistrates threatened them with jail or service in the Fleet if they would not take the wages offered them by the factory owners.

The *Warrington Guardian* of 1853 reports the case of a boy of 12 being charged before the Magistrates for leaving his employment as a fustian cutter, where he earned 4/6 a week and going to another cutter where he could get slightly better wages. The Magistrates released him on his mother promising to send him back to his original job. Again the following year it was reported that a boy of fourteen was charged with running away from his master. The boy contended that he did not earn enough to keep himself. His case was dismissed on his promising to return and pay expenses.

In times of industrial slump the workers' poverty and distress was deplorable. Many books have been written describing their living conditions in the new towns, and even ours did not escape these dark stains on its life.

Crowded together in narrow dismal courts and lodging-houses, in rows of soul-destroying houses, their lives were menaced by their unsanitary and unhygienic environment.

A Warrington slum courtyard in the late 19th century

In July, 1853, Alexandre Mackle wrote a letter to the *Guardian*, in which he says: *"Shopkeepers inform me their doorways are not their own after seven. From one back street not 50 yards from the main shops five hundred people will issue in a body on a Sunday evening and quickly cover the main streets."*

Much trouble was caused by the great influx of Irish peasant labourers who worked for cheaper rates, and who passed through the town from Liverpool in large numbers. They slept the night in lodging-houses, of which a writer to the *Guardian* of April 5, 1856, says: *"In Warrington there are two hundred registered lodging-houses crammed full, although registered for from 4-30 inmates each. Registration takes no real cognizance of damp cellars, crowded neighbourhoods, and contiguous or contagious middens."*

On July 16, 1853, the paper reports houses in Rose and Crown yard, near pig-sties, where liquid manure drains down the street for eight yards. On October 1 of that year it was reported that cholera was sweeping the county and that the open ditch, the depository of the town's filth running from Church Street to the Bridge, remained open as in 1832.

The Editorial for August 6 says: *"Squalor. and dirt reign in our streets,"* while a letter in the paper of the same date says that all hours of the day and night little children in rags and covered with dirt seem to be flitting through the streets. Another person writes that the poor children that daily meet our eyes have no religion, very seldom have heard of God, and any education would raise them a little.

On July 30th, says the *Guardian*, the whole of last Sunday evening the lower end of Buttermarket Street might have been said to have been in possession of the mob. For some time running fights went on between men and women in every stage of drunkenness.

Drunkenness was rife in the town. No. of public-houses and beer-houses in Warrington and Latchford in 1853, according to the *Guardian* of Nov. 5th, was 103. The beer-houses and gin-shops were often the worker's only means of forgetting for awhile his unhappy lot. The Chief Constable reported that for the ten weeks ending June 25, 1853, out of 323 charges 107 were for drunkenness.

Conditions, bad as they were, do not seem to have been so bad as in many other of the northern towns, and efforts were being made to clean up the town. On November 5, 1853, it was reported that the Warrington Improvements and Markets Bill - to pave, cleanse, light, watch, sewer, drain and otherwise improve streets, lanes, ways, widen Buttermarket, improve the markets and make several new streets - had passed its third reading. It became law the following year. In June, 1854, the Watch Committee recommended that the police force be increased to twelve men. It was assured that if they had a stronger force disturbances and riots would be prevented. One councillor recollected the time when they had only two policemen in the town.

Gradually though, as the years passed, conditions did improve. Various Factory Acts were passed limiting the hours of labour and forbidding the employment of children. Locally the Town Council steadily worked out a progressive policy. In 1852 they purchased the ancient market rights, so that through them it now truly belonged to the people for whom it was started so many years ago. Then in 1872 Bank Hall was purchased and made the seat of civic government. Gas works, water works, the museum and libraries were brought under public ownership.

Efforts to educate the young townsman were taken in hand. On July 21, 1855, the *Guardian* reported: *"It is the intention of our energetic Rector to commence at once a ragged school, in which the poorest of the poor will receive gratuitously on three evenings a week proper instruction in reading, writing, with the rudiments of plain English. On spare evenings the female portion will receive instruction in sewing, mending and patching. On Saturday evenings children will be supplied with decent clothing at Mr Quikett's cost, to be returned on Monday morning, and in this it will be required that they attend the Parish Church each Sunday."*

In 1857, Mr Morell, Her Majesty's Inspector of Schools reported as follows:--

Present ordinary attendance - Boys, 314; Girls, 110.
In 1880 the Town Council debated the state of education in the town. It was stated that in the previous year a School Attendance Committee was appointed to secure regular attendance of existing scholars and to bring in all waifs and strays. Its work was a failure. The debate lamented that the powers of the Act of 1876 were inadequate and that Parliament should invest the town councils with the powers of a School Board. Even as late as 1900 though, the *Guardian* reported that Horsemarket Street was usually the scene of small ragged barefoot newsboys, so hoarse that they could hardly speak and drenched with pouring rain.

Slow the progress may have been, but it was there nevertheless, and though much that was good of the old ways of life died in the quickening tempo of the industrial century, the times evolved for itself its own method of life.* The last years saw the town's life firmly established in the traditions of the Victorian age. A small wealthy set, a good respectable middle-class and a large poor labouring class. Bonnets and shawls with crinolines and bustles for the women; tall hats, high collars, frock coats, tight trousers, beards and side whiskers for the men. On the one hand the quiet dignity of the houses in Stanley Street, on the other the hovels of houses built round some one or others court. For the respectable the musical evening at home, for others the gin-shop with crowds of hungry children waiting outside.

*Some old customs still remained, as when a school inspector visited the town on Easter Monday and was lifted and kissed and carried round the town by a party of girls.- *English Custom and Usage*, Christina Hole, p.55.

Wars increased the industrial prosperity and sometimes brought fears of invasion. Then the people were united. Companies of defence volunteers were formed in the town, the Blue Backs of 1797, and the Robin Red Breasts of 1803, even as the Home Guard was formed in these days. Cessation of wars brought peace and sometimes trade slumps and much distress, but through all these years of endurance a new age was being born.

In 1894 the Manchester Ship Canal was opened, and with its building many landmarks of those days passed away. The Old Quay Canal was cut through at Stockton Heath, and the part from thence to Runcorn used no more except as a pleasant walk. The road to Chester along Greenalls Avenue ceased to be. The Mersey was joined to the canal at Walton Locks, revealing the old canoes of that other Warrington, and necessitating a river diversion, a straight cut alongside which the new Chester Road was made. Swing bridges and high level railway bridges appeared. Part of the river was cut off from the parent body and joined as a back-water to the canal. The river floods became a thing of the past, and its own dark waters no longer swirled through the arches of the Causeway.

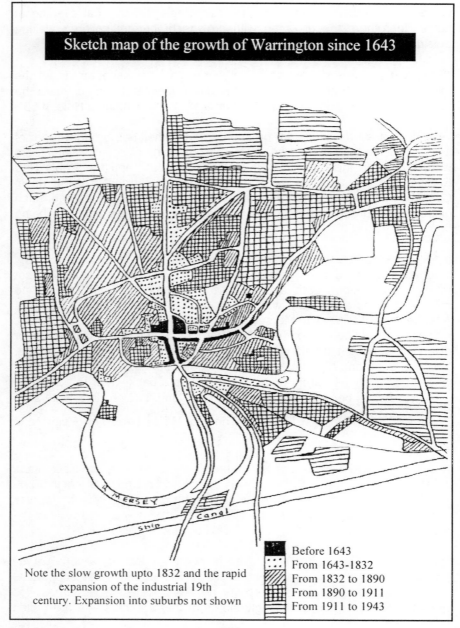

Sketch map of the growth of Warrington since 1643

R. MERSEY

Ship Canal

Note the slow growth upto 1832 and the rapid
expansion of the industrial 19th
century. Expansion into suburbs not shown

Before 1643
From 1643-1832
From 1832 to 1890
From 1890 to 1911
From 1911 to 1943

Chapter VIII
The Twentieth Century

The advancement in social conditions steadily improved. It can be safely said that more has been done for the town and its citizens during these last forty-three years of its existence than at any other period of its life, so that today it stands firm as the Gateway into Lancashire, and the Town of Many Industries.

In the last year of the nineteenth century the Warrington Corporation Act received the Royal assent, and on October 1, 1900, the town became a County Borough, an auspicious beginning to the new century.

Its steady increase in size is indicated by the population figures already given. Its long established industries continue to function, while the new age brings along its own activities till today its manufactures can be classed under the following main heads:

Agricultural Implements and Seeds, Aluminium, Bags, Baskets, Belting, Boilers, Boxes, Brewing, Bricks, Building, Cabinet Making, Cement, Chemicals, Clothing, Cotton, Electrical Goods, Files and Tools, Fustians and Velvets, Iron and Steel Goods, Margarine, Flour Milling, Motor Transport, Rubber, Soap, Spades, Tanning, White Lead and Paints and Wire Products.

During these forty years much has been done to take away the black spots of the last century. The narrow streets are widened, Bridge Street in 1908, Buttermarket in 1915. Others have still to be done. The new bridge was opened in 1913 and plays, and will continue to play, its part in the life of the town just as its less pretentious ancestors have done before it.

Parks and open spaces are provided for the recreation of its inhabitants. Labour hours and wages are brought into conformity with those acceptable alike to both employer and employed. New housing schemes are undertaken, and some of the ugly slums of that previous age are pulled down. Works buildings are brought into line with recognised modern conditions essential to the health and well-being of the worker. Following on the Education Act of 1903, the old National Schools, which had battled their best for the young life against prevailing conditions, are replaced by new schools, elementary and secondary, offering a wider and more varied vision to young people. Medical and dental, health and sanitary services now follow the young Warringtonian step by step along his path in life. A more varied and liberal culture is developing with the century's advancing years through the schools, the cinema, the library and the wireless.

Road traffice comes into its own again, though the garage replaces the old coaching inn, and through these cheaper means of travel the townsman comes to know more of his fellows elsewhere.

So we come to the end of our story. The geographical position is the same, though the present citizen's environment is different in its details from those of his ancestors. But basically the people are the same. His industrial skill comes to him from down the ages, from the pre-historic worker in bronze, from the Roman smith, and the mediæval armourer.

In times of peace he seeks a better life. The charter obtained by the citizens from the Boteler Lord of the Manor are akin today to the agreements made by the trades unions. The local bye-laws governing the building of the citizen's house are as much for his good as the mediæval tenant's charter whose clause states that he shall deposit no filth in the highway. In times of local and national distress he goes forth today just as yesterday. The lads of the wars of this century link themselves with those of the past, with the Blue Backs, with Sir William le Boteler and his retainers, with the Saxons of Thelwall and the Bronze Age men of Grappenhall. At all times it is their town, their hearths and homes, their heritage no less than their country that is in peril.

The proud traditions of the past, its life, sometimes ugly and dirty, other times of the best and good, pulsating down the ages, over years in number the mind can hardly comprehend, points to the citizens of today and tomorrow to go boldly forth in the future, to wrestle and strive, as they did, to the bettering of our home town and the fulfilment of its heritage.

May, 1942 - May, 1943.

Bibliography

Prehistoric Cheshire   W. J. Varley and J. W. Jackson, 1940

Prehistoric England   Grahame Clark, 1940.

Ancient England   Edmund Vale, 1941.

Everyday Life in Prehistoric Times   M. and C. H. B. Quennell, 1921.

Proceedings of the Warrington Literary and Philosophical Society.

A Lancashire Parish and its Life and History
                                              Rt. Rev. M. Linton Smith, 1919.

Warrington Roman Remains   T. May, 1898.

Roman Relies at Wilderspool   T. May.

Roman Cheshire   Watkins, 1886.

Roman LancashireThe Danes in Lancashire
                                              S. W. Partington.

The Saxon Chronicle.

Archæology of the Mersey District   Smith

Memoirs of Geological Survey - Geology of country round Chester
                                              A. Straham.

Geology of the Country round Liverpool
                                              G. H. Morton, 1891.

Mersey, Ancient and Modern   B. Blower, 1878.

Picturesque Cheshire   Coward.

Doomsday Lancashire and Cheshire   W. Beamont.

The Lords of Warrington   W.Beamont.

Victoria County History of Lancashire.

Lancashire Gazetteer   Clarke, 1830.

History of Lancashire   Baines.

Mediaeval Panorama   Coulton

River Irwell   J. Corbett.

An 18th Century Industrialist   Ashton.

Economica Vol. 15 Pin Making   T. Ashton.

British Isles   L. Dudley Stamp.

Geographical Basis of Lancs Cotton Industry, H .W. Ogden -
                                  Journal of The Textile Inst, Vol. 18.

Lancashire Pipe Rolls and Early Charters   C. W. Farrar, 1902.

Warrington Guardian Directory, 1908

Warrington Gazette, 1854.

Slater's Directory, 1895.

Oliver Cromwell   J. Buchen.

Leighs Lancashire, 1702.

Tour of Britain   Daniel Defoe.

The Years of Endurance   Arthur Bryant.

English Saga   Arthur Bryant.

Six Months' Tour of N. England   A. Young, Vol, III.

Economic History of Modern Britain   J. H. Clapham.

New Lancashire Gazetteer. 1830.

Historical Geography of South West Lancashire   Chetham Society, Vol. 103

History of the Commerce of Liverpool and the surrounding country
                                                    T.Baines, 1852.

Prehistoric and Subsequent Mining at Alderley Edge Chas. Roeder.

History of Lancashire   J. Croston, 1891.

History of Manchester and surrounding Country   J. Aikin, 1795.

Parys Mountain (Anglesey Antiquarian Society)   A. H. Dodd, 1926.

Journal of a Tour through North Wales   Arthur Aikin, 1797.

Report of Proposed Parliamentary Borough, 1832.

Conditions of the Working Class in England   F. Engles, 1844.

England in the 19th Century   A J. Freemantle.

The Town Labourer   L. H. Hammond.

Health of Towns' Commission. Report of state of Large Towns in Lancashire in 1845
                                                    Dr. L. Playfair.

Grappenhall   A. Hodgkinson

Transactions of Lancashire and Cheshire Antiquarian Society, 1883.

An 18th Century Journal   J. Hampdon.

Warrington in 1824   Baines

Universal Directory of Trade and Commerce and Manufacture, 1792.

Walks about Warrington   W.Beamont.

Retrospect of Warrington   W.Beamont.

Stockton Heath   J. Westbrook

Latchford   W.Beamont.

Early History of Warrington   Kendrick

Warrington Guardians, 1853-1943.

If you have enjoyed reading this book then you'll enjoy reading the following titles which can be ordered direct from the publishers.

A History of Golborne by J.E. Bridge £5.95

An Illustrated Guide to Jack the Ripper by Peter Fisher £14.95 (hardcover), £9.95 (paperback)

Jack the Ripper or When London Walked in Terror by Edwin T. Woodhall (limited edition) £10 inc. postage

The Sixpenny Rush by Tony Ashcroft £4.95 (A history of cinema in Leigh, Tyldesley and Atherton)

Chronicles of A Victorian Detective by Richard Jervis £3.95

Please send payment to P & D Riley, 12 Bridgeway East, Runcorn, Cheshire, WA7 6LD.
(make cheques payable to P & D Riley)

Look out for more new titles coming soon....

A RILEY LOCAL HISTORY PUBLICATION